Be Insurance Savvy

Home, Auto, Dwelling, Renter's, Flood and other Personal Insurance Explained

Lolita Scesnaviciute Guarin

Note: This book was created for educational purposes only. The author disclaims all warranties in respect to the representation of the completeness of the contents and accuracy of this book and should not be liable for damages arising from it. The examples, advice, and explanations mentioned in this book might not be applicable and accurate in all jurisdictions and situations. Different insurance companies or agencies might have a different opinion about the subjects mentioned. Any individual reading this book should contact an insurance agent for personal advice and professional service.

ISBN: 1475118708
ISBN-13: 9781475118704

Preface

Anyone who owns a vehicle or a home, rents property to someone, or possesses any personal items should have insurance to protect himself or herself from loss. I am a former insurance agent, and every day, I dealt with customers who were insurance illiterate. Not everyone understood, for example, that flood insurance was not automatically included with a homeowner's policy and end up financially hurt after the loss occurred. People need to understand the basics about insurance and protect themselves. They also need to know how to evaluate their insurance policies, because not all agents insure properly or even answer questions.

Insurance is a complicated subject for the average consumer. *Be Insurance Savvy: Home, Auto, Dwelling, Renter's, Flood, and Other Personal Insurance Explained* was created for anyone who wants to understand insurance better. This book will educate the reader about how to choose the right insurance policy, how to choose the right amount of coverage, and how to save money on insurance premiums yet still be properly insured.

The book is organized into seven parts, covering the basics of an insurance policy, liabilities and claims, home insurance, auto insurance, rental insurance, and other types of insurance. Each part explains the relevant points for each type of policy.

In this hard economic time, everyone is looking for ways to save money. Unfortunately, insurance expenses are understood as unnecessary loss of money, and some people cut back on those expenses. Learning what insurance is truly needed and understanding how policies work will save you money and give you peace of mind.

Table of Contents

Part I

Insurance and You

Introduction

In order to be properly insured, one needs an insurance quote from an experienced and reputable agent. It is very important to understand the process involved in looking for a good insurance policy as well as what personal information is used in determining an insurance premium. The tips below will help you become familiar with the steps needed to get an insurance quote and to identify a good insurance agent for professional service.

Chapter 1

What You Need to Know
Before Getting a Quote

For some reason, many people think that getting an insurance quote is so easy that it only takes one phone call, and they expect the results in five minutes. Do not expect the insurance agent to give you a quote at the end of the conversation. A good agent will create a custom quote just for you, giving you the best price the agency can offer.

Getting a quote and purchasing a good insurance policy is much more complicated than a quick phone call, and it is far from the "name your price" commercials. Since insurance is not a membership, do not be surprised if the insurance agent asks you all kinds of weird questions, many of which you probably have no answers for. Be prepared before you call the agent and embarrass yourself because you do not remember how big your house is or you are not sure when your wife's birthday is. Knowing what coverage you want also helps you get a more precise quote. Contacting one agent or one company and getting the first proposed policy is not the way to save money.

Here are tips and steps to guide you in getting a quote and having great coverage for your property.

Step 1: Gather all the personal information.

To get a precise quote, you will need to provide as much personal information about yourself or the other person you are getting the quote for as possible. Any information given to the agent is assumed true. Remember, insurance companies have their own ways to check the accuracy of the information you provide. Any intentionally or unintentionally misrepresented facts or omissions will change the policy later on. The insurance company has a right to change the premium, deny the risk, or cancel your policy completely.

Name

From the beginning, it is important to give the agent the legal name of the insured. Don't tell the agent that your name is Van, because your friends call you that, but on your driver's license it says Waldemar. The policy should list the correct name of an insured, so if a claim occurs, the check will be written to the right person. It is important to make sure it is done correctly from the beginning. When the check is on its way to you, that is not the right moment to remember that you used your maiden name on the policy and forgot to change it or that you got divorced and your ex-husband doesn't live with you anymore. Those changes need to be made immediately, or the check can't be cashed. Don't forget that if you have a mortgagee or lienholder for the car, house, or any other property and you don't completely own the property, the second insured on the check will be the bank that holds your loan. In order to cash the check, all insured need to sign the check.

Date of Birth

Date of birth of the insured or the drivers on the policy will make a big difference determining premium rates. Most of the time, insurance companies check the information by running reports. Date of birth can be the only difference between you and another person who happens to have a name similar to yours. You would not want to have the responsibility of the other person's claims, would you?

Different insurance companies have different ratings depending on the insured's age. Some companies prefer to do business with students; some prefer with more mature drivers. Many insurance companies give discounts to people older than 55. Teenagers are more likely to get into accidents and insurance companies increase premiums to compensate for future claims. Lower insurance rates come much later. Boys get a break when they turn twenty-five and girls when they turn twenty-one.

Social Security Number

Most people don't want to give their Social Security number to a person they don't know. Nevertheless, agents usually protect confidential information like that, so it is safe. Some people think that running their Social Security numbers will hurt their credit scores. It is not true, because insurance is not applying for a new line of credit. Running your Social Security number does not hurt your score. It creates what is called a soft hit. The electric company also runs your credit score before it provides service to see how likely you are to pay on time. Actually, having a great credit score can save you money on insurance.

When asking for a quote, look up your or your spouse's credit score and ask the agent to put the name of the person with highest score first on the policy. The information for the first named person will determine the policy premium. A spouse or other family members can be on the policy and named as additional insured. When you receive the policy, make sure your spouse's name is listed as insured. If it is an auto policy, make sure all the children who drive are listed. Homeowner's, flood, or other insurance don't need to list all residents. They only list the persons with a financial interest in the property.

Mailing and Property Address

The correct mailing address is important for communication between you and your insurance company. Insurance companies still send any changes or questions about the policy, any checks, and communication from the adjuster by mail. When you move, please update your mailing address with the agent. If you have a couple of properties, let your agent know where you wish to have your policy documents sent.

Your property's location is the most influential factor that determines whether the insurance company will insure your property. Insurance companies have a map to group the risk areas. Insurance companies avoid some areas because there is a greater possibility that claims will occur in that area more than they occur somewhere else. Based on the statistical data, the insurance company determines high-risk, catastrophic loss, or high-crime areas.

Some insurance companies have had so many claims in the past that they decided to control their losses by not insuring properties in a high-risk zone. Therefore, if you hear your agent say, "Your ZIP is closed," it means this particular insurance agency is not writing new business in your area. Look for another insurance company who is interested in your area. Depending on their financial books, insurance companies open and close different areas for new business all the time. If last year this company was not insuring new business in your area, don't assume that this year they are not taking any business either. Always check with your agent.

If the area is high in crime, your insurance premium will be higher than in the other part of town where crime is low. That is why most people are confused when they see that moving from one part of the city to another changes their auto rate.

Education

The insurance agent also will ask you about your level of education and your current occupation. It makes a difference on your insurance rate. Insurance companies think that people that are more educated are less inclined to have an accident and are more responsible, so the company will face fewer losses. Insurance companies like employed people, especially if they have a high-paying occupation. It all might look too intrusive to you, but all the insurance company cares about is that the premium will be paid on time and that they will have fewer losses to pay.

Family Pets

It might not look strange to you when your agent asks if you have a swimming pool with a fence. Having a pet should seem not to be an insurance company's concern. It is. The type of pet—the breed of dog, a monkey, an alligator, or a snake—can influence your acceptance by the insurance company. Not many insurance companies accept vicious animals on the premises. Families with pets statistically have more liability claims that insurance companies want to avoid. Some insurance companies do not take new business when the insured has a particular breed of dog; some make the insured sign an "animal exclusion" form stating that any liability claim from having this pet will not be paid. After the policy is issued, an inspection is usually done on the property, and the inspector will notice the pet on the premises. It is a good idea to tell your agent ahead of time that you have a pet so the policy is not cancelled.

- For an auto quote, the agent will ask:
  * Where your car is garaged
  * Your driver's license number. Please don't be afraid to give this information to the agent. They will not steal your identity. It will save you time and allow you to get a precise quote.
  * The year, make, and model of the car. The agent will not need to know the color of the vehicle or the license plate number. In the insurance world, things like that do not count. Moreover, for the record, a red vehicle receives the same rating as any other vehicle.
  * It is a good idea to give a VIN (vehicle identification number) to the agent. A claims report will be run at the time the quote is prepared, and the rate will be more accurate.
  * If you added something to your car that was not there when the car came out of the factory, you should insure it. Gather receipts to prove to the insurance company how much your car should be insured for special equipment, which includes stereos, rims, carpets, and any other custom upgrades to your car.

* Think about how far you drive to work. Is it about five or fifteen miles per day one-way? Depending on the company, you might be getting a discount.

▶ If you are looking for a homeowner's quote, be sure you know all the property information, such as:
  * The age of the house.
  * The construction type of the house (frame, brick, or stucco).
  * The number of stories.
  * How many bathrooms the house has.
  * Whether there is a pool or a trampoline.
  * Whether the garage is attached or detached.
  * Whether there are additional structures on the property, such as a shed where you keep the equipment to take care of the house.
  * Whether there is an apartment above your garage.
  * Whether there are any patios, canopies, decks, or awnings or any unusual masonry or stonework.
  * The type and age of the roof, water heater, and furnace.
  * If the house is more than twenty years old, the agent will ask you when the plumbing and electrical systems were updated.
  * Is your home custom built? Have you had any additions or remodeling recently done to your home?
  * You should know how far away the fire station is located and how far the nearest hydrant is from your home.
  * Don't forget to provide alarm information. A certificate will be required, and you will get a discount.
  * Do you have home business?
  * Do you have any dogs, alligators, monkeys, or other pets?

At some point, it will seem that the only thing the agent did not ask about was your shoe size! Answer every question. The more information the agent knows, the better the quote the agent can prepare for you, customized to your needs.

For home, auto, health, or life quotes, make sure you know your claims history for at least the past five years. Don't try to hide that information or lie about it. Don't joke, saying, "Tickets? Oh, I thought you meant real tickets, like to the movies or the game." Every insurance company runs a claims report before issuing a policy. It is a good idea to know your current coverage, deductibles, and premiums. Give that information to the agent. Don't say, "Oh no. I won't tell you anything. I don't want you to lower the price to suit my current limits!" There is no way that an agent can "adjust" the price. If that were possible, all insurance agents would adjust the prices to benefit themselves. If you have your current policy handy, show that to the agent. You will get an accurate, apples-to-apples quote. If you are shopping for a quote online, your current policy declarations page will give you good reference numbers to input.

Step 2: Ask for a referral.

Ask trustworthy friends and family if they know a good insurance agent. Ask them how long they have been dealing with the agent. Don't forget that insurance is not a membership. There is not a fixed rate for everyone. Rates vary from person to person. Even if you have the same house as your neighbor, factors such as your credit score, claims history, age, and education can make the rate higher or lower.

Step 3: Decide which type of agent you will use.

There are three types of agents: exclusive, direct, and independent. Agents are discussed more in Chapter 2.

Step 4: Think about coverage and deductibles.

Dwelling limits on a homeowner's policy are based on a replacement cost estimator; every insurance company uses its own estimation. That is why it is possible to get different dwelling limit quotes from different companies. Remember, dwelling limits are how much the insurance company will pay to rebuild your home, not how much your home is worth now or how much you can sell the house for. Therefore, if an insurance company says that your house should be insured for at least $340,000, you can't lower the limits. However, you always can get higher limits on your house and personal property than the replacement cost. If you remodeled your home, insure your house for more than the regular builder's grade estimator does. If something happens to your home, at least you will cover the renovations and the amount of money you put into a house.

Higher deductibles can help you reduce premiums because the higher deductibles lower the premium. When getting quotes from different agents, pay close attention to deductibles. Some agents like to use high deductibles to get your business, but when the loss occurs, you have to cover a big repair bill. Be careful. Calculate how much you can afford to spend on repairs if a loss occurs. Don't think that because there was no hurricane in the area for three years in a row, you can increase your deductibles so much that you will empty your savings account if you ever have to pay.

If you are not sure about which deductible to choose, ask the agent to give you a couple of quotes with different deductibles.

Step 5: Set aside some time.

Set aside time to invest in contacting the agents, calling insurance companies, and researching insurance on the Internet. Don't put it off for too long—every day counts when you can be saving on insurance. Getting an auto quote at least eight days ahead of the effective date will get you a discount.

Step 6: Get as much information as possible.

When you talk with an agent, get as much information as possible. Use your current insurance declarations page for comparison. Ask any question that comes to your mind about the quotes and about the company the agent wants you to insure with.

Step 7: Compare quotes.

After you gather as many quotes as you can, compare all of them. Choose two or three quotes that look the best. You should check the policy coverage limits, deductibles, and prices. Then look closer at the company giving you the quotes. Don't believe everything you read on the Internet, especially websites that start with the insurance company name and end with "sucks." Obviously, people who write those websites are upset. Have you ever heard of anyone starting a website about things that went right? I would recommend going online and checking their rating with your state department of insurance. Pay close attention to consumer complaints and the claims record, because you will be dealing with these areas if you file a claim.

Do not favor companies that you heard of or have seen commercials for on the television. Different insurance companies deal with marketing different ways. Some insurance companies just don't invest money in advertising because they leave advertising to their agents. If you have never heard of the company, but the ratings, coverage, and prices are good, look into it.

Step 8: Contact the agent.

After you decide which quote you want to go with, contact the agent who gave it to you. If the policy comes back with a higher or lower premium, ask why. If you are not happy about the way this particular company handles your policy, you always can move to another quote that you liked. Remember, you have the right to cancel your insurance any time you want. There is no need to wait until the expiration date.

Chapter 2

About Agents

Every day, we face major risks that can cause financial ruin: damage to our houses, auto accidents, medical bills or lawsuits, disability, premature death, or extended long-term care. Unfortunately, we are not aware of these risks. We pay for insurance and complain that we pay for something that we don't use.

Sadly, many of us learn about the importance of insurance only when we get in trouble. There is no insurance class taught at school, so many of us learn about insurance as we go from news reports or hear insurance horror stories from our family and friends. If you are already paying for the insurance, why not be insured properly? That is why you need to make sure you have a great agent who can give you recommendations for any life situation—an agent who knows you when you call. You want someone who greats you with, "Hey, Scott. How are you? How is that new car you bought back in July?"

When you invest, you don't want to hold all your eggs in one basket. In insurance, the opposite is true. It is a good idea to have all your policies with one agent so the agent knows how to insure you properly to suit your needs. A good agent will take care of all policies and make sure any change in the family situation will be reflected in all policies you hold. A good agent will educate you, answer all your questions, and give you advice.

Types of Agents

The agent is a link between you and the insurance company, and you should choose that link wisely. Just because your best friend is an agent doesn't mean that he will take care of you. If the agent finds you the best price for an insurance policy, it doesn't mean he will do well with servicing that policy in the future. Agents are different not only with the quality of services they offer, but also because the kinds of agents can influence that quality. They are not all created equal. There are three types of agents: exclusive, direct, and independent.

Exclusive or "captured" agents are agents who write with Allstate, Farmers, State Farm, and other big insurance companies you have heard of and have seen on television commercials. Those kinds of agents write business only with the company they work for and are very limited in providing a variety in premiums and coverage. Therefore, if you are not happy with your premium that has risen on renewal, you are out of luck. In addition, many big companies write business under their names but are business partners with other insurance companies. You might get a quote with one company, but the actual policy is with the other company.

Direct agents are employees of companies that allow you to call directly using an 800 number. They will give you a quote the same day, often at the end of the conversation. Geico and Progressive are two examples of this type of insurance company. It will take some time to call each company to get a quote, but if you have time, direct companies will save you some money because there is no agent between you and the company, and you are saving on commissions. Depending on what is more important to you, the premium or the service, you can choose to go directly with the insurance company you choose. However, if you want personalized service, you won't get it. Each time you call to the company to submit a claim or ask a question, you will speak with a different representative each time and will need to repeat your story all over again to a different person.

There are insurance companies that will submit a claim for you as soon you call in to ask just a simple claim question. Even if the claim is rejected, it is still stays on your record. So be careful whom you call. When you deal with insurance companies directly, you will not get advice about your personal situation. The same person will not follow up on your claim to make sure it was handled properly and can't recommend a roofer with plenty of experience in your area. There is no personal touch, just a lower premium for the same coverage.

Independent agents deal with more than one insurance company. They have much more ability to compare a quote with the same coverage and shop for the best premium, saving you time and energy. An independent agent will shop for a better price on renewal and transfer you from one company to the other without you doing anything. The agent will contact your mortgage company for you, provide evidence of insurance for you, and make sure the renewal premium is paid. Independent agents know your personal situation, have the history of your previous companies and claims, and can recommend which way to go.

When you want to submit a claim, always call your agent for advice. Some might argue that by having an agent you spend money paying the agent commissions. Ask yourself what it is more important to you. Is it that you save $50 a year, save more by getting advice, or save by not submitting a claim that could cause your premium to increase? A good agent will follow up on your claim and have better contact with supervisors. Because they are independent, they understand the importance of bringing a value to you to have you as their client for many years to come. If you are not happy with the way your insurance company handled the claim, or if the insurance company is constantly increasing your premium, an independent agent will shop for you and give you the best quote without wasting your time and without you having to give your personal information all over again.

Finding an Agent

Now that you know about the types of agents, there are a couple of ways to reach the agent you need to sell you a policy. Different people prefer different ways. If you don't like talking with people or don't like to leave the comfort of your home, the Internet will give you many options. There are websites that give you quotes depending on what information you entered. Just go to Google and type "homeowner's insurance quotes" to get plenty of websites to help you with that. Just remember that you will need to talk with someone eventually. The agent still needs to review quotes received through the Internet. There are websites where you enter your information, and the information is forwarded to different agencies in your area that e-mail or call with a quote. Using the Internet will save you time.

If you are a people person, you will want to meet the agent responsible for your policies. That way, you can see what the agent's office looks like as well as who is working for the agent. Any of your questions about the quote and coverage can be answered right there. Of course, if you have more than one agent, visiting in person will take time and effort.

Usually, not many people visit their agent. With today's technology, all business is done by phone, fax, and e-mail. Policies are sent to the insured by e-mail to sign, payments are done online, and claims are submitted by phone. Many agents don't keep paper documents in huge filing cabinets anymore. Many insurance companies are trying to cut paper and mailing expenses by encouraging policyholders to sign up for paperless documents and by giving a discount on the policy if they do.

There are many ways to get a good insurance policy. Moreover, if time is what you have the most of and shopping for a good policy with reasonable premiums is important, then go try them all.

Agent Qualifications

When you call your insurance company, most of the time, you will not speak with the most experienced agent there. If you are calling directly to a company 800 number, a different person answers the phone each time you call. For any problems or difficult questions, always ask to speak directly to the agent.

Agents are required to complete continuing education classes every year. Nevertheless, the good agent will get more education than required. Courses agent can take to improve their education include:

- ▶ Certified Insurance Counselor (CIC)
- ▶ Chartered Property Casualty Underwriter (CPCU)
- ▶ Accredited Advisor in Insurance (AAI)
- ▶ Certified Life Underwriter (CLU)

For a list of agents completing the above-mentioned courses, go to the CPCU Society at www.Cpusociety.org or the Society of Certified Insurance Counselors at www.cic.com. If nobody recommends a particular insurance agent but knows a good insurance company, go directly to the company. You can find that kind of information by calling the company directly or searching the Internet. Every insurance company lists the most experienced and accomplished agents in your area.

Agent Commissions

Understanding how agents are paid can be a factor in how you select an agent. In most states, insurance agents get the same commissions on the policy, from ten to fifteen percent. The good news is that all agents get the same commission percentage, but the bad news is that this is so no matter what policy they sell you and regardless of their experience level, skill level, or the quality of the service. They are paid the same. That is why it is very important to get an expert agent.

Service

Purchasing an insurance policy provides not only coverage, but also policy service, professional advice, and all the help you can get. These are important considerations. It will not make any difference how high or low your premium is when a claim needs to be filed. You will need someone to guide and help you. Your insurance agent should have yearly reviews with you about every policy you hold to avoid coverage gaps because you do not want any surprises when you file a claim.

When you add a youthful driver to your auto policy, the agent should recommend an umbrella policy; when you buy a new home, an agent should remind you about flood coverage. The agent should watch your back. If the big loss occurs that damages your home and auto, you need to make only one phone call! It is better to look for an agent who is an expert on every type of personal insurance you need: home, auto, boat, flood, medical life, long-care, and any other coverage that you might need in the future. It is not recommended to have more than two agents on different polices.

Here are some things agents can do:

- ▶ An agent should give you advice as to what claims to file and what losses to cover yourself. Just remember, the agents are not adjusters, and they don't deal with claims, so don't be disappointed if your agent can't answer some of your claim questions.
- ▶ A good agent will call the adjuster and get the answers for you.
- ▶ A good agent fights for your rights during the claim and goes the extra mile in communication between you and your claims adjuster.
- ▶ The agent makes sure that the amount paid to you is the right amount and makes sure the check is delivered on time.
- ▶ A good agent always has ways to resolve a problem by contacting a claims supervisor or somebody else higher on the ladder.

Remember, you should always pay attention to your deductibles, which is how much you will need to pay out-of-pocket at the time of loss. It is always better to pay extra on the policy but sleep well at night knowing that you don't need to clear your savings if a hurricane comes through. There are agents who look only for low premiums and are pushing for sales. They will give you a low premium, but the deductibles are high.

When you chose the quote you want, take the time to be sure the agent selling you the policy is a good fit for you. Don't be afraid to ask about the agent's background, such as the agent's educational level, practical experience, and years worked in insurance industry. Make sure that you trust your policies to an agent that will contact you regarding any change in your policy, and do yearly reviews to make sure you are insured properly with no gaps between your policies. Your agent will always notify you when insurance premiums change and will make an effort to shop for better premium for you. It is important that the agent has enough experience with claims and will be a strong advocate for your rights during the claim. More than that, the agent should know about the quality of service and financial strength of any insurance company that he or she does business with.

Chapter 3

The Process of Getting Insurance

After the agent gets the information to do **a quote,** he or she submits the information to the insurance company for underwriting review. Some agents call the insurance company directly. Most of the time, it is done through software that specializes in preparing quotes for different insurance companies.

Some insurance companies reject your application based on their specific underwriting guidelines. If the company accepts you, the agent presents a quote and will explain details about the coverage, deductibles, and payment options. You can accept or reject them.

When you agree to purchase the policy, the insurance agent will issue **the binder** and give you the **application** to sign. Please don't think that if you do not sign the application, you don't have insurance. Usually, applications are created after the agent issues the binder. Every application has your policy number, which is assigned after the policy is issued. Make sure you understand what coverage you are getting and your duties as the insured before you give your permission to issue the policy. Ask as many questions as possible.

If you notice mistakes on the application, please tell your agent. Most of the time insurance companies generate the application only once, so don't expect the agent to make a new application just because you remembered that your wife has a higher education than you said she had before. Mistakes on the application can be fixed with a simple endorsement.

Once the agent issues the binder, you have insurance coverage. The binder gives temporary coverage until the policy is issued. It is effective up to ninety days. Nevertheless, before the actual policy is issued, the insurance company checks your personal information to make sure that the company wants to deal with you.

Insurance agents have numerous resources for checking the accuracy of the information that you are giving to them, but insurance companies have even more ways to measure you. Underwriters have an access to inspection services; government bureaus, such as the Bureau of Motor Vehicles; financial information; and previous insurance and claims information. So if you lied to the agent and he could not catch it, the underwriters will.

After the policy is issued, an inspector from the insurance company goes to the property to make sure that is insurable. On renewal, some companies reinspect the dwelling. After it verifies your personal information and history and inspects the property, the insurance company still can decide not to issue the policy and cancel your binder.

When a policy is issued, a **certificate of insurance** or evidence of insurance should be submitted to the mortgage company's insurance department. If you are buying a house, the lender will require you to have it on closing day or before that to calculate closing costs. When you are buying a vehicle, show the salesperson evidence of insurance.

If you change insurance companies, it is very important to notify your mortgage company or lien holder about the change. Accordingly, when you change mortgagees, you should notify the insurance company about that also. If the mortgagee does not get evidence of insurance on renewal from the insurance company, it will assume that you don't have insurance coverage, and the bank will force-place insurance on you. That will cost you three or four times more.

In many cases, if you already have insurance, you can respond with evidence of insurance or contact your agent immediately to help you with that matter. The agent who services your policy will do it for you, and there is no need to notify your mortgage company about a change. Some mortgagees require authorization from the insured to change the insurance company and make a premium payment from your escrow account. The agent servicing your policy will let you know if you need to call your mortgagee to authorize the change.

You always have responsibilities for the property you are insuring. You can't abandon the property if it is damaged. You can't walk away from the burned house and say that it is your insurance company's responsibility. Bankruptcy of the insured doesn't relieve the insurer from the responsibilities under the policy.

Part II
Anatomy of an Insurance Policy

Introduction

After you found a good insurance agent and choose the quote, it is necessary to understand the process that will take in getting actual policy. Knowing how to read your policy, understand the coverage and terminology used in the policy will give you peace of mind and prepare you for easier reading when your policy arrives in the mail.

Chapter 4

What Is Insurance?

L et's begin by defining common terms.

- ► **Agent** is a person who is authorized by insurance company to solicit applications, collect premiums and write policies.
- ► **Insurance** is a transfer of a risk from the insured—the person purchasing the insurance—to the insurance company, which is the entity selling the insurance. The insurance company can help you repair or rebuild your home, reimburse you for stolen items from your home or vehicle, and even pay medical expenses arising out of unfortunate events that cause injuries to your guests while they are on your property. It doesn't insure the property; it insures the person who owns the property. Insurance cannot make you money. You can't insure the property for more than the insurance company thinks your property needs to be insured for so you can make a profit.
- ► An **Insurance policy** is a contract between the insurance company and the insured. It is a consideration in exchange for a premium

that can be done only between two competent people. A minor, a person under the influence of drugs or alcohol, or someone who is insane can't sign a contract. Signing the policy **application** means you are signing a legal agreement between you and the insurance company. You agree to pay the premium to the insurance company. For that, the insurance company agrees to compensate you for your lost property and belongings. Depending on the property you own, the insurance coverage will provide you financial assistance in the unfortunate event when your property is damaged or stolen.

► **Property** is anything a person buys or anything with his or her name on the title.

► **Insurable Interest** or **Insured** is the person who has financial interest in the property. You can pay for your parent's homeowner's insurance or your child's auto insurance, but you can't collect a check from the insurance company if you are not the one on the title. If you still need to pay the bank for your auto or home, the mortgage holder owns your home and has financial interest in the property, same as you. There are two important categories for this definition: additional insured and first named insured. **Additional insured** refers to people who have a financial interest in the property but who are not first on the policy. A mortgage or lien holder and your family members are listed as Additional Insured on the policy. Although there may be many names on the policy, there is only one first named insured.

► **Policy forms** provide coverage for kind of property that you own, such as a dwelling, vehicle, boat, personal property, etc. **Blanket form** covers the same type of property in different locations by a single amount of coverage. It also can cover different property at a single location.

► **Losses. Direct losses** are damage caused by a covered peril directly, including rain, lightning, fire, and others. **Indirect losses** are losses incidental to the direct loss. For example, if you have a broken pipe somewhere in the wall, water damages the floor of your house and while the repairs are made, you cannot live in the house. You have to go to the hotel and eat meals at the restaurant. The insurance company will reimburse you for your hotel stay and meals because you were affected by indirect loss.

▶ **Peril** is a cause of loss. **Named Perils** are perils listed on the policy. If it is not listed on the policy, it is not covered. **Open Perils** means the opposite, which is that the policy covers every peril except those listed as exclusions. Open perils is the coverage you want. For more information about perils, please read Chapter 23.

▶ **Deductibles.** A **deductible** is the agreed amount of loss that the insured needs to pay before insurance company will pay the rest of the loss. The declaration section of the policy shows the amount of the deductible. It can be indicated by percentage or the actual amount. Insurance companies use deductibles to limit small claims by the insured. Increasing deductibles lowers insurance premiums.

▶ Like any other contract, insurance policy also has **exclusions**. No insurance company covers maintenance expenses. Therefore, if your car rims need to be repainted or you ruined your car engine because you were not changing oil on time, insurance company won't cover the loss. Losses like that are called non-accidental, and includes everything from tear and wear, rust, deterioration, corrosion, scratching, chipping or breaking mechanical breakdowns of lack of maintenance. Those kinds of losses are controllable by the insured and it is the duty of the insured to take care of the property.

▶ **Extra-hazardous perils,** such as flood, are not covered by default but can be insured separately per insured's request. Catastrophic losses such as war are also not covered, because that would cost the insurance companies a huge amount of money or even a bankruptcy. In addition, the items one policy covers cannot be covered under another policy. That would be called double coverage and is not permitted. So even though your auto is your property, it should be insured separately under auto insurance. Read the exclusions in a policy carefully before purchasing the policy.

Chapter 5

Choosing Policy Limits

E very insurance policy comes with certain limits. **Policy Limits, Limit of Coverage**, or **Limit of Liability** on the policy shows how much the insurance company is going to pay for the total loss of the property.

Personal auto policy limits should be chosen depending on the vehicle the insured drives, the experience of the driver, and liability limits higher than required state minimum.

A dwelling limit on your homeowner's insurance policy is not the amount your house is worth on the market now, and it is not the actual amount of your loan. An insurance company calculates the dwelling limit by using replacement cost estimators. Every insurance company has its own replacement cost estimators, so don't be surprised when different quotes have different dwelling limits.

The dwelling limit is how much it would cost to rebuild your home if you suffer total loss. Let's say your house burned down. If you have no less than or equal to 80 percent of the full replacement cost of the building at the time of the loss, there is no deduction for depreciation and losses are paid on replacement cost basis. For example, let's say Ed's home has a replacement value of $100,000. To have the home rebuilt at replacement cost, Ed should carry insurance that is equal or greater than 80 percent of $100,000, making it $80,000. If loss occurs, the insurance company will pay only up to the insured limit or $80,000. If Ed doesn't have proper coverage, such as less than 80 percent, the insurance company will pay the larger of a proportion of the replacement cost or the actual cash value of the loss.

In the event you submit a claim, the insurance company will use the different types of replacement cost to determine how to pay you.

Replacement cost is the actual amount of money it would cost you to buy a new thing. There are items in the household that cannot be calculated with replacement cost estimators, such as your **personal property**. For your personal items, insurance companies list an agreed amount for the property in the policy. It is important to insure your personal property using replacement cost, not the actual value calculation.

Actual cash value gives you replacement cost minus depreciation. So if you bought a leather couch ten years ago for $3,500, don't be surprised that the insurance company is giving you only $350. That is the depreciated value, and you don't want that method used on your policy. For expensive, unique things, such as jewelry, art, or musical instruments, it is a good idea to use a separate schedule for them on your homeowner's policy. You will need an appraisal to show to the agent. But when the item is on the policy, and it is lost or destroyed, the insurance company will pay the amount indicated on the appraisal. It is important to reevaluate your items and get new appraisals every couple of years.

A **proportional replacement cost** is calculated by dividing the amount of insurance that the insured is carrying by the amount that he is required to have. Then the result is multiplied by the amount of the loss. The formula looks like this:

$$\frac{\text{Insurance carried} \times \text{amount of loss}}{\text{insurance required}} = \text{amount of reimbursement}$$

For example, let's say Ed's home has a replacement value of $100,000, but he has only $50,000 in coverage, not the $80,000 he should have. The loss is $16,000, so by the formula, Ed will get only $10,000 from the insurance company.

$$\frac{\$50,000 \times \$16,000 = \$10,000}{\$80,000}$$

If two or more insurance companies provide same coverage for the same property, the primary insurance company will pay for the loss first. It should pay up to the limit of the limits of the liability or until the loss is paid. When the first insurance company pays for the loss and exhausts the primary coverage limit, the second insurance company needs to cover the rest amount of the loss. For example, let's say Alice has two separate dwelling policies covering the same perils—that is, two different insurance companies cover the same property. The Policy A limit is $40,000, and the Policy B limit is $60,000. Alice has the loss valued at $20,000. If both policies use a pro data method to pay for the loss, then Policy A will pay $8,000, and Policy B will pay the rest, $12,000.

Understanding the limits listed in your policy is one of the most important items to understand, because it directly affects you if you have to make a claim. If you do not understand something in your policy, ask your agent until you do understand.

Chapter 6

Policy Parts

Most policies consist of four parts: declarations, insuring agreements, conditions, and exclusions. Because every insurance company has its own way of doing business and presenting the policy to the insured, those parts can be put in a different order than described here.

- ▶ **Declaration** pages list information about the insured: the name of the person insured or their legal representative as well as the insured's date of birth, driver's license number, occupation, and mailing address. It also has information about the policy itself, such as a description of the property insured, where the property is located, lien holder or payee information, amount of coverage that the property is insured for, and the premium that the insured needs to pay to keep the coverage. It also includes policy effective dates, deductibles, and a list of endorsements that alter the premium. Sometimes endorsements are at the end of the policy, depending on the insurance company.
- ▶ **Insuring Agreements** describe the actual property covered under the policy in more detail and explains the perils it is insured against,

such as fire, lightning, hurricanes, etc. To find out more about perils, please read Chapter 12. The **definitions** section explains terminology used in the policy. Words are usually presented in bold or quotation marks. This part of the policy sometimes has its own part, depending on the insurance company.

▸ **Conditions** describe the rules that the insurance company and insured will follow. Policy conditions address issues such as duties in the event of the loss and how the claims will be settled and valued. It describes the mechanisms for resolution what would happen in case of a disagreement between the insurance company and the insured. Any conditions mentioned in the policy are a matter of the law of the state where the insured's property is located.

▸ **Exclusions** describe the losses that insured is not covered against. Those are policy provisions that restrict, define, or limit the coverage. Insurance companies use exclusions for a couple of reasons. It could be that the exposure is not insurable by the insurance company—for example, flood insurance. Maintenance or warranty items are also excluded. There are risks or exposures that the average person won't be normally exposed to, such as owning an aircraft, or the excluded item can be insured by other specific insurance policy, such as boats, or business insurance.

Chapter 7
Life and Death of Insurance Policy

E very insurance policy has a beginning and an end. The **policy period** or term, is the period between when the policy goes into effect and when the policy expires, usually at midnight. There are different term policies: six months, a year, three years, or other. Policies renew automatically on the renewal date as long either party do not cancel it. A policy can be canceled at renewal or in the middle of the policy term.

There are different reasons an insurance company can **cancel** the policy. It depends on the insurance company, and each state requires different cancellation procedures. Please check your policy to make sure you understand this provision.

An insurance company can cancel a policy without reason within first sixty days of the policy. It should give ten days' written notice to the insured. After sixty days, the insurance company can cancel the policy only with reason. If the policy is being canceled due to misrepresentation by the insured, a thirty-day is notice required. If the reason for cancellation is a substantial change in risk, the company has to notify the insured thirty days before cancellation takes effect.

If the insured did not pay for the policy, the insurance company will cancel the policy and give ten days' notice. Upon cancellation, the unused premium—called **Unearned Premium**—is refunded to the insured. The insurance company can't keep the extra amount for expenses, and the refund is calculated on a pro rata basis.

The insurance company also can not **renew the policy** for numerous reasons, such as: too many cancellations, constant non payments of the policy, or many claims. Or the property is in a bad shape and repairs have not been done on the timely matter or not complete at all, insurance company can not renew the policy. An insurance company considers a dwelling to be in bad shape if any of the following exist: broken fences, tree limbs on the roof, missing shingles, rotten trim and window frames, exposed wires, or other repairs that need to be made. If the property is in a bad shape, the insurance company usually gives the insured a chance to complete repairs. They send a detailed letter listing the specific steps that insured needs to follow to keep the coverage. After the repairs are done and the insured sends a signed letter and pictures as proof of the repairs, the insurance company usually renews the policy.

The insured can cancel an insurance policy without any reason, at any time during the policy period. With most policy types, there is no need to wait until the policy expires to cancel it. Nevertheless, please, check with your agent. A signed letter or verbal cancellation directly to the insurance company or the agent should be enough to cancel the insurance policy when the insured wants to. Some insurance companies require proof of other insurance or documents indicating the item was sold to cancel the policy. Different agencies process cancellations different ways.

Chapter 8

Endorsements

E very homeowner's, tenant's, or condominium unit policy can be similar and different, depending on the insurance company. We all have different things and have different needs. Standard home-owner's, renter's, or condo policies are sometimes not enough to satisfy a particular insured's needs. Some insurance companies can include a particular coverage to the policy automatically, and some require an endorsement be added to the policy.

Numerous possible endorsements can be added to your policy. Just ask your agent to help you to choose the right endorsement for you.

Coverage C: Scheduled Personal Property Endorsements

Homeowner's insurance covers many personal property items, but in some cases, certain risks for which the insured will require coverage are not. An insurance policy has exclusions and limitations for certain types of property that are particularly susceptible to loss, have high value, or are difficult to value. Personal property items can be insured under a scheduled personal property endorsement, which is also called Coverage C.

Scheduled personal property endorsements provide coverage for nine optional classes of personal property: jewelry, furs, silverware, fine arts, stamps, coins, musical instruments, cameras, and golf equipment.

This type of coverage provides open peril coverage against any kind of loss, even mysterious disappearance. Although some things are excluded, such as war, nuclear hazard, wear and tear, gradual deterioration, inherent vice (a condition of defect that exists within the property), vermin, and insects. This coverage is not subject to a deductible.

When the item is stolen or damaged, the insurance company will reimburse the insured for the actual value, cost of repair, or cost to replace with a substantially identical item or with an amount of insurance specified in the policy, whichever is the lowest.

Scheduled personal property endorsements are subject to the **pair of set condition**, which states that the insurance company will not be liable for the entire value of the set when only part of the set is damaged or lost. The set can be repaired, replaced, or restored. Or the insurance company can pay the insured the difference between the actual cash value of the full set and the actual cash value of the undamaged part.

Generally, the insurance company requests the insured to submit an **appraisal**, and if it is possible, color pictures of the item. The appraisal is helpful determining the coverage limit for the item. Appraisals need to be updated every three to five years to make sure they are up to date. If you add the items and forget about them for ten years, it could be that the coverage limit is too low at the time the claim is made.

Scheduled personal property endorsements automatically cover certain classes of newly acquired property when the property is in a category of property that is already insured, such as in a class of furs, jewelry, cameras, musical instruments, or works of fine art. For all property except fine arts, automatic coverage applies for the first thirty days after acquisition, and the property is covered for 25 percent of the applicable limit of insurance or $10,000, whichever is less. For fine art, coverage applies for ninety days and is provided for up to 25 percent of the applicable limit of insurance. For newly acquired property coverage ceases after thirty or ninety days unless the insured notifies the insurance company about the property during this time.

Sometimes, it is better to keep expensive items, especially those with sentimental value and those that are irreplaceable, in a safe deposit box. Some high-value personal items, such as jewelry, can be insured by a separate policy.

Personal property replacement cost endorsements allow the losses to be settled at replacement cost rather than by actual cost value, without taking into consideration the depreciation. The insurance company will pay the insured the full repair cost of the damaged items or enough money to replace the damaged items if it is impossible to repair it.

Other Endorsements

Other endorsements include the following.

- ▶ **Permitted incidental occupancies endorsements** provide coverage for the insured's business activities conducted on the residence premises. This coverage is usually excluded under a homeowner's policy. The endorsement also covers other structures on the property used for business purposes. This covers anything the business uses, such as equipment, furniture, and supplies. This endorsement adds liability coverage and medical payments in connection with the described business on the policy. Let's say you have a daycare business. This endorsement will give you more coverage, and the premium of the policy is based on the number of children being cared for.

- ▶ A **business pursuit** endorsement provides liability coverage for a business conducted away from the residential premises. It is good coverage for people who teach, are in sales, or do clerical work. This endorsement is not for business owners. Business owners should purchase a separate business liability policy.

- ▶ **Personal injury endorsements** modify the bodily injury coverage to include personal injury to the policy, covering items such as slander, libel, invasion of privacy, malicious prosecution, wrongful entry, and false arrest.

► **Mobile home endorsements** can be added to the homeowner's policy for mobile homes that are tied down, with tires removed, and are at least ten feet wide and forty feet long.

► **Earthquake endorsements** can be added to the homeowner's policy per an insured's request in the areas where earthquakes are possible. Any aftershocks within period of one week are considered one accident. Coverage is subject to a deductible.

► **Watercraft endorsements** provide coverage for watercraft up to twenty-six feet long and powered by an outboard engine or motor exceeding twenty-five horsepower. An endorsement is also used to cover sailboats more than twenty-six feet long.

► **Limited fungi, bacteria, and dry or wet rot endorsements** add coverage for liability and property losses arising out of fungi, wet or dry rot, or bacteria. This kind of endorsement is for HO-3 and HO-5 policies only. It covers the cost to remove the mold from the property and the cost to tear out and replace any parts of the building or other covered property as needed to gain access to the mold. Coverage only applies if the loss or cost resulted from covered peril that occurred during the policy period. In addition, the insured should have done everything to prevent the property from further damage when the covered loss occurred. In other words, if a hurricane hit and you did not look to see that your roof was leaking, and two years later, you get into the attic and see that there is mold, you are not covered. The most the company will pay will be the scheduled amount, no matter how many claims and occurrences there are.

► **Sewer backup** covers damages caused if liquids back up from sump pumps, sewers, and drains. The coverage limit can be as high as $10,000 or even higher, depending on the company.

Chapter 9

Words You Need to Know

n addition to the parts of a policy, there are terms that you will need to know when purchasing insurance.

▶ **Death of named insured.** If the insured listed on the policy dies during the policy term, a legal representative will become the insured with a regard to the insured property listed in the policy. Policies like that are issued with "in estate of..." on the policy.

▶ **Concealment or fraud.** If any information provided has been wrong, the coverage is not provided to the property. Concealment must be intentional in order for the insurance company to void the policy. Let's say Bill requests a homeowner's quote from the agent but tells the agent that his home is used strictly as a residence. He does not tell the insurance agent that he is baking cupcakes in his kitchen and sells them online. If the insurance company finds out that he is manufacturing something in his house, he uses his home for business and the insurance company has the right to cancel the policy all together. He should have gotten a business endorsement on his existing homeowner's policy or have a separate commercial policy.

- ► **Liberalization clause.** Liberalization clauses give additional coverage without an additional premium charged. The insurance company decides to broaden the coverage and apply it automatically to the policy.
- ► **Waiver of change.** This means that the policy must be in writing or it is not valid.
- ► **Assignment.** One person cannot transfer their policy and coverage to the other insured without the written consent of the insurance company.
- ► **Subrogation.** This is how the insurance company recoups money that it paid to the insured for the claim. The insurance company goes to collect the claim money from the responsible party's insurance company. Let's say your neighbor's son breaks your window, and your neighbor's insurance refuses to pay for the window. You will submit the claim to your insurance. The insurance company will pay, and then your insurance company will go after your neighbor's insurance company to get the money for the loss.
- ► **No benefit to Bailee.** No coverage will be provided to anyone who is storing, moving your property for a fee, or just holding your property. For example, dry cleaners, tailors, or movers who destroy any of your property will not be covered under your homeowner's policy. They have to have their own insurance policy and will be liable for that loss.

Part III

Liability and claims

Introduction

When a person injures another and damages another's property, the person is liable for losses. The liability portion of the policy covers the insured against those losses and protects the insured from financial catastrophe. It is important to understand how to choose the right liability limits, how to submit a claim, and how to act after the loss occurs.

Chapter 10
Liability Coverage

A common conception is that all of us should live in peace with each other and care about each other. A prudent person would never do something that will endanger another person. Most of time, we have no idea we are endangering someone.

There are so many situations in life where we assume responsibility without knowing the many things that can go wrong. For example, let's say you are hosting your mother's golden anniversary and are ordering food from a local, family-run restaurant that everybody loves. Do you know that you assume all the liability for the injuries to guests if somebody spills a drink and slips on the floor? Do you know that food poisoning is also your responsibility, even though it was your favorite restaurant providing the old seafood? You need event insurance so you don't end up paying for the defense cost of the restaurant in any injury lawsuit out of your own pocket.

When person injures someone, damages someone's property, or violates the law, the person is liable for the losses to be paid. Insurance companies provide **liability coverage** to protect you against lawsuits. The bodily or property damage incurred in an accident or continuous and repeated exposure to substantially the same harmful conditions must occur during the policy period.

Types of Damages

Compensatory and **punitive** damages are two types of damages. Compensatory damage can be a specific, very precise loss measured in dollar amounts of the loss, such as funeral expenses, medical bills, lost wages, and so on. Let's say Lonnie got into an accident and broke her leg. The medical expenses will be considered specific compensatory damages. General damages are impossible to measure, such as the pain and suffering of a person. In the previous example, Lonnie got into an accident, and because of her broken leg, she has a big scar on her leg and is not feeling comfortable wearing short skirts. She can ask for general damages for her suffering.

Punitive damages also called **exemplary damages** and are caused when a person willfully, on purpose, causing bodily injury or property damage to the other person. Punitive damages are awarded to punish the person who did it and make an example to show that such behavior will not be tolerated. Many states don't permit insurance companies to pay punitive damages, so to be sure, check with your agent.

Types of Negligence

Negligence is a common concept for insurance companies. Many times people do things without thinking that somebody can be harmed. **Negligence** is an unintentional civil wrongdoing, and a liability policy will cover those damages. **Tort** is a civil wrongdoing against other person, and it is the most common basis of negligence. **Intentional torts** are called criminal cases, and Insurance companies do not cover them.

For an insurance company to pay a negligence claim there should be bodily injury or property damage loss due to the insured being negligent. For example, Frank has a patio in the backyard with a rotten wooden bench. Frank should have thrown the bench away a long time ago and replaced it with a new one, but because he had no time, or for some other reason, the bench is still there. His neighbor Patty comes for a visit. Patty sits on the bench, the bench falls apart, and she ends up on the ground. Because of this accident, Patty breaks her hip and is rushed to the emergency room. Frank's homeowner's policy will pay for Patty's medical bills, X-rays, and other expenses due to Frank being negligent. If Patty were to fall but not injure herself, and none of her clothing was damaged in the accident, then there will be no claim to pay.

If the person was negligent himself, for example, ignored the wet floor warnings, and caused accusations of negligence toward the other person who cleaned the floor, the claim will not be considered negligence.

An **accident** is an unintentional, unexpected, or unforeseen event or chance occurrence that happens at a fixed place and time. **Repeated occurrence** is the loss caused by continued and repeated exposure to the same conditions over time.

Assumption of risk is when a person assumes the risk, voluntarily and with knowledge of potential danger. The insurance company will not pay these claims. For example, Chang went to the basketball game, and a ball hit him in the face. He cannot sue the owners of the team for his medical bills. By going to a sporting event, Chang assumed the risk and could have avoided the harm by not going to the event or watching the game on TV.

If you are dealing with **hazardous operations** or dangerous animals or are involved in dangerous activities, you are considered to hold **absolute liability**. Even if the case does not include negligence, dealing with those kinds of hazards makes you liable, and the insurance company will not pay those claims.

Limits of Liability

Depending on the type of liability, there are two types of limits: per person and per occurrence.

- ▶ **Per person** liability limits show the greatest amount that will be paid to one person per accident. Mostly, this type of liability limit is used in a personal auto policy.
- ▶ **Per occurrence,** limits are the most that an insurance company will pay for the loss, no matter how many people are injured in the

accident. In a homeowner's policy, per occurrence can mean the specific action at the specific time, only once, such as when there's an accident or broken window. It can also mean the duration of time that the cause occurs, like if leaking water from an insured's pipes damages the downstairs neighbor's ceiling.

In a personal auto policy, the limits are divided among all persons who submitted a claim by equal parts until the liability limit is exhausted. For example, Jackie has an auto policy with bodily injury limits of $30,000 per person and $60,000 limits per accident. Jackie caused an accident, and two people were injured. Jaime claims $25,000 losses and Kim claims $30,000. Jackie's policy will pay $25,000 to Jaime. Kim will receive only $25,000, even though the limit per accident is not exhausted, because the limit per person is exhausted. The rest of $5,000 will need to come out of Jackie's pocket.

There are different kinds of limits.

- ► **Aggregate limits** are how much money will be paid per policy term, no matter how many people are involved or how many times an accident or claim will occur.
- ► **Split limits** refer to the limit divided between bodily injury and property damage. They are most commonly used with personal auto policies. For example, a personal auto policy has limits of bodily injury per person, per accident and a property damage limit.
- ► **Combined single limits** are mostly used for liability policies. Combined single limit is very flexible and covers bodily injury and property damage. Using the example mentioned before, if Jackie had a $60,000 combined single limit policy, Kim's claim of $30,000 would be paid in full with nothing left Jackie to pay out of pocket.

Why We Need Liability Insurance

Liability insurance provides benefits to the insured, such as paying the claim payments, providing defense, and covers defense costs. The insured needs to cooperate with the investigation, and the insurance company will hire the attorneys and investigate the claims. The terms of the policy obligate the insurance company to provide a defense for any covered claims described in the policy. If the policy does not cover a claim, the insurance company is not obligated to provide the defense.

In different states, there are different laws about the statutes of limitations and time when particular lawsuits must be filed or they lose validity. Usually, the claims can be submitted within two years from the time of occurrence, but please check with your agent.

What to Do if Someone Makes a Claim Against You

Whatever happens, never admit liability. Never give any money or make any payments to the person without the knowledge and consent of your insurance company. Any payment, even a very small one just to "help them out," will count against you and will be construed as admitting liability. After the incident notify your insurance company immediately and let them know what happened in detail.

Your insurance company will hire a lawyer to defend you. If you hire your own lawyer, the insurance company can decline to pay your lawyer's fees. Do not discuss the claim or the lawsuit with the person making a claim or that person's attorney. Make sure you keep all the copies of all letters and legal documents sent to you. Any documentation the insurance company asks for needs to be sent as soon as possible.

Chapter 11

Your Duties after Loss

When you sign a contract and enter into an agreement with the insurance company, the insurance company has **duties to perform**, and so do you. Read your policy to understand what your insurance policy is covering and what it is not covered as well as what your deductibles are. Read all endorsements because they alter the policy.

If you don't understand something, contact your agent or insurance company directly to answer your questions. Knowing your policy will help you to make a decision about whether to submit a claim. Overall, you should know that you have to take care of your property and maintain it at all times. If you have not taken care of the property and maintained it well, the insurance company has a right to decline your claim. After the loss occurs, as an insured, you have duties that the insurance company is expecting you to perform.

First, you should protect the property from additional damages. If you fail to take action, the insurance company can pay less for the loss after determining that loss could have been smaller if you would have done something to prevent it or protect it. For example, if a window is broken during a storm, board it up or cover it with something that prevents more rain from coming inside. Or let's say you got in an accident, and your convertible roof will not close, but you still were driving in the rain when you didn't have to, even though you knew that rain was damaging the car further. The insurance company will pay you to repair the accident damage, but it won't pay for the rain damage.

If you went to the store and bought needed materials to prevent further damage, the insurance company reimburses you for it. Keep the receipts and write a short note to indicate what those materials were used for.

Before you start removing debris and making changes to a scene, take pictures so you can show them to the adjuster later. Do not throw away damaged property; wait until the adjuster comes to see it. If you throw away the evidence, you won't be paid to buy a replacement!

It is a good idea to have an **inventory list** with a listed value for everything that you own before the loss occurs. That way you don't have to think about what you had or how much it was. This helps the adjuster assess the loss and move faster with the claim. It is hard to remember what you have at the time of loss. If you think that you don't have that much, just remember how much it costs to go shopping to the store for couple of things. It can add up fast.

At least once a year, you should go around your house or any other property and take pictures of the things you own. Take pictures of everything in the closets, drawers, and boxes. Store the pictures or the DVD of the film in a different location, but not in your house, because if a hurricane hits and all your property is out into the open, the pictures will not be found. Store the evidence in your office, in the bank, at your friend's house, or somewhere where you can access it when you need it. You also should keep receipts of expensive items you bought or repairs that you have made. Also record any additional living expenses that were incurred due to your inability to live at your home after the loss occurred.

Report the loss to the insurance company as soon as possible, preferably in writing. If you are involved in a claim and injured other person, you should contact your insurance company and give written notice as soon as possible. The injured person can submit their records to the insurance company and submit it to the doctor the insurer selects. Never make a payment to the person who submitted a claim, because by voluntarily making a payment you are acknowledging that it was your fault.

Signed and sworn proof of the loss should be submitted to the insurance company within sixty days of the insurer's request. The term can be extended, but it should be confirmed in writing. When you write to the insurance company, mention the time and cause of the loss, the inventory of damaged, destroyed, or lost property, specifications of damaged buildings, and repairs that have been done to the property. Include any receipts for any additional living expenses incurred and records that support the receipts. The insurance company needs to know if there is other insurance that may cover the loss, if there are other insured's or liens involved on the property, if there any changes on the title, and the occupancy of the property during the term of the policy.

Don't delay submitting a claim and repairing the damage to your property. That will just increase the damage. Most of the time, the insurance company will accept claims made two years after an occurrence. So if the hurricane came three years ago, and you just now noticed that you have mold in the attic, the insurance company will decline the claim because you did not report it within a reasonable time.

Part IV

Insuring Where You Live

Introduction

T he most expensive item people will purchase in their lifetimes is a house. Home, be it a single family home, a condominium, or a townhouse, is where the majority of monthly income is spent. Losing a home in a fire or receiving wind damage can be devastating without proper insurance. Anyone who has a homeowner's policy should understand what it covers, how high the limits are, and how premiums are determined.

Chapter 12

How Homeowner and Dwelling Premiums Are Determined

When you are shopping for a new policy or renewing old one, it will help to know how insurance companies determine **premiums**. Insurance rates determine policy premiums. Rates are generated by analyzing statistical data about various individual information and risk factors.

Insurance is not a membership. Not everybody pays the same amount, so you can't compare to your parents, friends, or neighbors, even if they own a house exactly like yours. Every insurance company has its own factors in setting your premium. These are called underwriting guidelines. Some insurance companies have preferred areas for accepting risk. Sometimes, after a big loss in a particular area, such as a big hurricane, the insurance company has a high number of claims. Then this company increases premiums to recoup money it has lost. Sometimes the company even leaves the state completely!

Here things that insurance companies use to determine your premium for homeowner's, auto, renter's, and other policies.

1. **Amount of coverage.** The higher the coverage limits, the higher the premium. Mortgage companies require you to have property insured at least up to the loan amount you owe. But they cannot make you have insurance higher than the limits of the replacement cost the insurance company provided. Insurance companies calculate coverage limits based on a replacement cost estimator, and that is the minimum coverage limit you should have. Your land is not covered. It is recommended that you increase the coverage limits every year on your property, and usually it doesn't cost that much to do so. It is better to have more insurance than less.

2. **Amount of deductible.** The deductible is the portion of the claim amount that you must pay before the insurance company will cover the rest of the claim. The higher the deductible, the lower the premium, regardless of the type of policy. By paying the deductible, you assume a higher liability, leaving the insurance company to pay less. Deductibles for auto insurance usually range from $100 to $2,000, depending on the company. Homeowner's insurance deductibles can be from $1,000 to 1 percent of the insured value of your home. There are agents who write policies with 2 percent or 5 percent on hazard deductibles to keep the premiums low. Be careful if you are choosing a high deductible. It can save you money when you pay your premium, but it can be painful to pay that 5 percent of the dwelling limit out of pocket when the time comes. If you have wind and hail coverage on your home, your policy will have separate deductible just for that. Depending on the state, wind and hail deductible can start at 1 percent of your dwelling coverage limits and go as high as 5 percent.

3. **Location.** Insurance companies have a code for every territory. Insurance companies favor some areas over others. There are zip codes that companies don't take new business at all. The subdivision you live in also determines your premium. Is your subdivision gated? Do you have a live person to let you through the gate?

Does your house have an ocean or river view? What about the climate? Is it hot or cold?

4. **Credit score and personal profile**. The better your credit score, the lower your premiums. Insurance companies, like any other company, check your credit to predict possible nonpayment cancellations and claims. Just don't be scared to give your social security number to the agent, especially if you have a high score. It does not "hit" your credit. It hits your credit only when you are applying for a loan or trying to increase your line of credit. Otherwise, insurance companies, as other company inquiries, are called soft hits and don't hurt your credit score. If you have a low credit score, the insurance company can decline coverage or use it against you as a factor for high premiums. There are still companies that don't run credit reports, so it is important to shop around and find those companies. You can save hundreds of dollars.

5. **Claims history**. If you had any claims from your previous residence, it will count against you, and your premium will be high. The more claims you have, the higher the premium. If the claim was nature-related, such as a hurricane, strong winds, or a tropical storm, the insurance company will not count it against you. Insurance companies don't like theft claims, especially if you have had a couple of them in the past. It just shows that you have a history of thefts, and you probably will continue having them. From the insurance company's financial standpoint, they will experience more losses than profits having you insured with them. Different insurance companies take the age of claims into consideration, sometimes going back three, five, or more years, depending on the company.

6. **Construction of your house**. How old is your house, and when were your electrical and plumbing systems updated? Some insurance companies don't like houses more than ten years old; some don't like when the home is built on a crawl space. Every insurance company has their own preferences. Is it built of wood

(frame), or is it brick veneer (masonry)? Is the builder an accredited builder who used fire-resistant and noncombustible materials?

7. **Protection.** Does your house have smoke detectors? Maybe your home has a sprinkler system? If you have these items, you can get a discount on your policy. Just don't confuse a fire protection system with a sprinkler system for your grass in your backyard. Do you have a fire extinguisher at the house? How far is the nearest fire hydrant and fire station? Is your roof hail and wind-resistant? Do you have an alarm system? Is it monitored? Check with the insurance company; you can get a discount on all of these items.

Chapter 13
Homeowner Policy Basics

Anyone with financial interest in the property and lives there should have a **homeowner's policy**. If insurance company declines this coverage, person can insure the property with Dwelling policy.

No matter how many people own the home, there can be only one primary named insured. All other insured's, such as a spouse, other residents of the household under age twenty-one in insured's care, and the lender, are considered additional insured's. So if you are renting a room to someone who is not your relative and is not in your care, such a boarder, he or she does not qualify as additional insured and is not covered under your homeowner's policy.

According to a homeowner's policy, a home cannot board more than four families, one additional family, or two roomers. So if you sister decides to move in with her kids until she gets herself a new husband, watch out. Insurance companies do periodic inspections and can cancel your homeowner's policy. The more people living on a property, the higher the liability.

A homeowner's policy is a multiline policy and is a package of different coverage. It provides coverage not only for your personal property, but also for dwelling coverage, other structures that are on the property, loss of use, and liability. The policy comes as a package, and you cannot exclude any of its parts. If you want to insure your property for liability only or for personal property only, it should be insured with a different policy, such as dwelling or tenant policies.

A property cannot be vacant for more than sixty days, or the insurance company will cancel the policy. Even though it looks as you are the owner of the house and you do as you please, when nobody lives there and something happens to the house, the losses can be huge. There are a few reasons a property can be vacant:

- ► If the property is purchased and being renovated and nobody lives there, it should be insured by a vacant property policy.
- ► If the property is being sold and is not rented out, it should be also insured with the same vacant property insurance policy.
- ► In case of a parent's property being vacant and for sale because the last parent passed away, the property should be insured by a vacant property policy. The first named insured on the policy can be named "in estate of" the parent.
- ► If the house is being built, it is unlivable yet, and a builder's risk policy should be purchased before the construction is more than 50 percent complete. That way, all the building materials on site are covered.

Farms and mobile homes need their own policies because they cannot be covered under homeowner's insurance. A mobile home is insured with homeowner's insurance only if the policy is altered with a mobile home endorsement.

Your home cannot be used for businesses purposes, except for certain incidental occupancies such as private schools, day care, studios, and offices, and only with business special endorsement coverage added to your existing homeowner's policy.

If you are not sure what insurance policy you need to get, please refer to Figure 1 for help.

Figure 1. What insurance policy do you need?

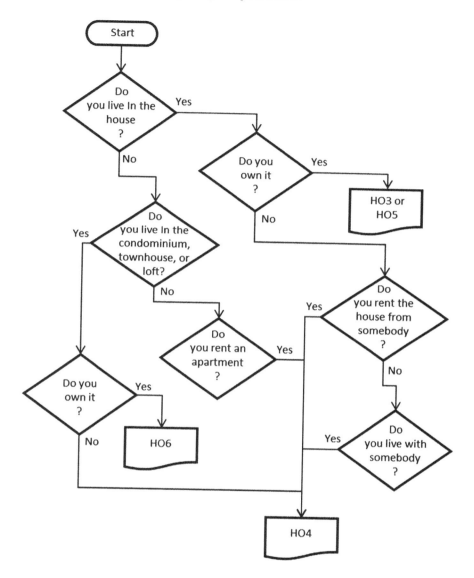

You and Your Mortgagee

If you still owe money to the bank for your home, depending on the state you live in, you have a **mortgagee or lender** who holds your trust deed as the security interest on your home loan. Your lender requires you to have insurance because it has a financial interest in your home to the extent of the unpaid loan balance. That is why your bank is always listed as an additional insured up to the day that you pay off your loan. Having no loan to pay means a discount on most homeowner's policies.

Your lender always needs to be informed about your insurance policy and the specifics of that policy, such as what company handles your insurance, the policy number, and the effective date of your policy. If you do change your insurance provider, your mortgagee needs to know about it immediately. Since the house also belongs to them, as additional insured, the bank needs to protect its property. Your mortgagee wants to make sure that you have proper insurance coverage all the time. If you forget to pay your insurance policy and it is cancelled for nonpayment, your mortgage company will receive a cancellation letter from your insurance company. If you don't have an active insurance policy with another provider, your mortgage company will **force-place** insurance on you.

You never want to have insurance force-placed on you for several reasons. Most of the time, force-placed insurance is much more expensive—double or triple—the insurance policy that you can get from the insurance company yourself. The banks do have affiliates or a subsidiary with the insurance company they use and make money out of it. Most force-placed policies provide very limited coverage and favor your lender, not you. Depending on the policy, none of personal property or liability can be insured under policies like that. And what is the point having insurance if it doesn't cover you?

Some insurance companies send evidence of insurance to mortgagee, but some fail to do that. Make sure you notify your lender about your insurance policy change as soon as possible.

Sometimes, an individual can act as a mortgagee. The investor or the owner of the property can sign an installment contract with a person who lives in the property. The person who enters that kind of a deal promises to pay every month to the investor until the loan on the property is paid. The investor or the owner of that property should be added to the homeowner's policy as additional insured until the loan is paid. For example, Leroy's brother Stephen owns a house and wants to sell it. Leroy wants to buy his brother's house, but unfortunately, his credit score is very low and none of the banks will give him a loan. Stephen doesn't need to have all the money for the house right away, so he makes a deal with his brother without involving the bank. Stephen will be an additional insured until Leroy ends up paying for the house in full.

Homeowner's Policy Forms

There are six homeowner's policy forms:

- ► HO-1 (HO 00 01) provides basic coverage.
- ► HO-2 (HO 00 02) provides broad coverage for the dwelling and personal property. It is similar to DP-1 with extended coverages that cover breakage of glass and theft, vandalism, and malicious mischief.
- ► HO-3 (HO 00 03) is a special form providing open peril coverage for the dwelling and other structures. It is the same coverage as HO-2 for personal property.
- ► HO-4 (HO 00 04) is a broad form and does not cover a dwelling. It is good for renters and tenants. It provides broad coverage for personal property, with the same coverage as HO-2 and HO-3.
- ► HO-5 (HO 00 05) is a comprehensive form that provides open peril for both personal property and the dwelling. Remember, open peril means if it is not excluded, it is covered.
- ► HO-6 (HO 00 06) is a unit owner's form that provides coverage for those who live in a condominium or townhouse. It has broad coverage for personal property and very limited coverage for the dwelling itself.
- ► HO-8 (HO 00 08) is not available in many areas anymore, and it is basic coverage on dwelling and personal property. It was for older homes that far exceeded their market values and came only with replacement cost coverage. This form covers only against the basic perils.

Coverage A and Coverage B are discussed in more detail in Chapter 14 and Chapter 15. For the list of perils covered under Coverage A and B of these policies, please refer to Table 1 below.

Table 1. Homeowner's Policy Coverage (Coverage A Dwelling and Coverage B Other Structures)

Perils Insured Against	HO-1 & HO-8 form	HO-2, HO-4 & HO-6 form	HO-3 & HO-5 form
Fire or Lightning	Yes	Yes	Yes
Windstorm or Hail	Yes	Yes	Yes
Explosion	Yes	Yes	Yes
Smoke	Yes	Yes	Yes
Vehicle	Yes	Yes	Yes
Aircraft	Yes	Yes	Yes
Theft	Yes	Yes	Yes
Vandalism	Yes	Yes	Yes
Riot or Civil Commotion	Yes	Yes	Yes
Volcanic Eruption	Yes	Yes	Yes
Falling Objects	No	Yes	Yes
Weight of Ice, Sleet, or Snow	No	Yes	Yes
Accidental Discharge or Overflow of Water or Stream	No	Yes	Yes
Sudden & Accidental Damage from Artificially Generated Electrical Current	No	Yes	Yes
Cracking, Bulging, or Burning of Heating System, Air Conditioner, But Not Water Heater	No	Yes	Yes
Freezing	No	Yes	Yes
Theft to Dwelling under Construction	No	No	No
Vandalism if Vacant More Than Thirty Days	No	No	No
Tear, Wear, Mechanical Breakdown, Rot, Rust, Pollution, Insects, Animals, Etc.	No	No	No

Chapter 14

Coverage A, Dwelling

Coverage A covers the main residence the insured owns and lists on the policy. The insured property should be listed in the declarations page. Coverage A of a policy insures the **main building** and attached structures, such as an attached garage or porch. It also covers construction or repair supplies next to the insured property. For example, it covers lumber bought to build a porch and stored in the backyard. Coverage A does not cover the land that the dwelling is standing on. Newly bought residences, temporary residences, premises rented for nonbusiness use, vacant land, cemetery plots, and burial vaults are also covered.

Other structures not connected to the main building and standing completely separate, such as a detached garage or swimming pool, are insured under Coverage B. To find out more about other structure coverage, please read the next chapter.

It is very important to have a high enough dwelling limit to cover the total loss of the property. Insurance company underwriters, the group of specialists who are responsible for determining the rating and eligibility of the property, have all kinds of supporting information to help them make sure the property is insured properly. Examples include the materials that were used to build the dwelling, the materials and the age of the roof of the structure, materials used to finish exteriors and interiors, insulation, adequacy of heating system, plumbing and electrical systems, number of fire divisions in the structure, number of stories, and bathrooms.

A **replacement cost estimator** determines the dwelling limit on your policy—the limits that your property is insured for. Replacement cost is the amount of money that the insurance company will need to pay you to completely rebuild your home in the event of a total loss. Every insurance company has its own formula to determine the number that your property should be insured for and most of the time will not insure it for less. This number has nothing to do with appraisal estimates or market values. The sales price of real estate also cannot be taken as dwelling limit, because the sale also includes the land.

If you decide to rebuild your home yourself, to replace it just as it was before the loss, it could cost you much more than doing it through a builder. Large builders purchase materials at much better prices from the suppliers because they buy more. Don't forget that you will need to pay architect fees and other expenses.

There are six general forms of replacement cost coverage:

1. **Actual cash value.** This coverage is calculated by taking the replacement cost at the given time minus depreciation. The dwelling can be replaced or repaired with like or equivalent construction, up to the dwelling limit.

2. **Building code upgrade coverage.** This coverage repairs or replaces the damage to the insured dwelling with additional coverage for the costs to build a dwelling to current building codes as of the time of rebuilding. This coverage is mostly used for very old dwellings that are not built up to the current building codes.

3. **Replacement cost.** This covers repairs or replaces the damaged dwelling with like or equivalent construction. It replaces up to the policy limit but requires that the dwelling be insured for at least 80 percent of its replacement cost at the time the loss occurred.

4. **Extended replacement cost.** This coverage also repairs or replaces the damaged or destroyed dwelling with like or equivalent construction, but it is subject to a specified percentage or amount in addition to the insured dwelling limit. This type of coverage can be up to 50 percent, and different insurance companies have their own calculations. Please check with your agent. This type of coverage is used to cover big reconstructions on the house, such as a four-bedroom addition. Simple things such as remodeling your kitchen, replacing countertops, or painting the walls are considered maintenance or wear and tear items and should not be considered as additional costs.

5. **Guaranteed replacement cost.** This kind of coverage will pay for the full amount that is required to replace the damaged dwelling with the equivalent construction. It does not cover the additional cost to rebuild the dwelling up to the current codes. This kind of policy needs a review every year to make sure it has enough coverage for those upgrades.

6. **Guaranteed replacement cost with full building code upgrade coverage**. This will cover everything up to the additional cost on the policy. Not all insurance companies have such coverage, and if direct agents can't help you, look for an independent agent who works with more than one insurance company.

All forms of replacement cost cover the repair or replacement with like or equivalent construction. It is intended to put you back where you were before the loss occurred, not in a better position. If you decide that you want to have better materials or you want to upgrade your kitchen floor tile, the insurance company won't pay for the upgrade. Consult your agent about how high your dwelling limits should be. Document your agent's answer. In case of loss, if you do not carry the right coverage, and the insurance company leaves you with the additional costs, you can submit a complaint against the agent. You should show documentation where the agent was advising you about the wrong amount of limit and indicate you were relying on it.

Coinsurance Clauses and Inflation Guards

Coinsurance clauses are included in homeowner policies to make homeowners insure the property close to the replacement cost value. Ideally, all properties should be insured 100 percent, but the most common coinsurance requirement is 80 percent. To be sure, check with your agent. It can differ depending on the state. If the coverage is not sufficient, the insurance company can penalize the insured. If the loss occurs and the property is insured for less than 80 percent, the insurance company will not pay for the total amount of the loss because the property was not insured properly.

Inflation guard is usually built into the policy to offset the construction cost for the future losses, and it is used at certain time intervals. That is one reason a renewal premium is higher than last year's premium. If you keep your homeowner's or dwelling insurance policies insured with the same company for many years, it could be that the replacement cost amount is far higher than it needs to be. Depending on the company, it can be a 1 percent, 2 percent, or 3 percent increase in the dwelling limit. Not all insurance companies do that; some leave this decision to the insured. Please contact your agent and go over the replacement cost estimator. That way, you will make sure that your property is insured properly. For example, Liz has a homeowner's policy that increases the dwelling limit every year. All other coverage on the policy also increases, increasing the premium to pay. Over the last ten years, Liz's dwelling coverage increased more than $80,000. Liz had no remodeling and no upgrades done to the house and believes that her property is insured too high. She called her insurance agent and updated replacement cost details about the house. If the replacement cost estimator comes in lower than Liz's dwelling limit, she can request a lower limit in writing.

To find out more about the covered perils and exclusions, please go to Chapter 23.

Chapter 15
Coverage B, Other Structures

Coverage B covers **other structures** separated from the main dwelling by clear space or connected only by a fence, plumbing, utility line, or similar connection. Other structures include:

- A detached garage
- A shed in the backyard to store a lawnmower
- A barn
- A guest cottage located on the insured's land
- A gazebo
- A greenhouse attached to the porch of the house
- Fences, driveways, and walkways
- In-ground swimming pools

By default, other structures are insured up to 10 percent of the Coverage A dwelling limit. For example, Sybil's house is insured up to $200,000. Her Coverage B limit is 10 percent by default, which makes it $20,000. Depending on the insurance company, per the insured's request, the coverage can be lowered or declined all together. Since Sybil has no other structures, she can chose lower the coverage to $5,000, which is just enough to cover the fence, sidewalk, and driveway. Lowering the other structure coverage limit will also lower the premium.

The land the other structures are located on is not covered. If the other structures are rented to any person not a tenant of the main dwelling, it is not covered. If the garage is rented to use as a garage, there is an exception. For example, Tanisha has a house that has detached garage. She decides to rent the garage out to her neighbor, who will use the garage to keep his Ferrari. In this case, the garage is covered under Tanisha's policy. But if she rents the garage to store her friend's furniture, then the garage is not covered.

None of the structures are covered if there is any kind of business conducted or if the structure is used to store business property. For example, Davis is a plumber that runs his business from the shed located in his backyard. In this case, a commercial or business insurance policy is required. Although depending on the business, a business endorsement can be added to homeowner's policy to give some protection to personal residence. With the special endorsement, a barn rented to a friend to use as a retail art store is covered, as are other business purposes, such as hairdresser, day care, or other incidental occupancies. Ask your agent about endorsements that permit business use. Depending on the company, more options might be available.

To find out more about the covered perils and exclusions, please go to Chapter 23.

Chapter 16

Coverage C, Personal Property

Everyone has personal things that should be insured properly in case of a loss. **Coverage C** provides coverage for **personal property** belonging to the person listed on the policy and household residents. Personal property is covered against named perils on that specific policy, subject to a deductible.

Homeowners sometimes are confused as to which personal property is covered under Coverage C. Clothing, stamp collections, and granite countertops in the kitchen all belong to the insured. Imagine if you were to take your residence and flip it upside down. Anything that would fall out of it is considered your personal property. In the example, clothing and a stamp collection would be considered personal property and would be covered under Coverage C. The countertops in the kitchen would be covered under Coverage A, dwelling coverage.

Usually, personal property covers up to 50 percent of the dwelling amount. When the quote is generated, all coverage is calculated by default. Some insurance companies have personal property insured up to 50 percent, and some go up to 60 percent of the dwelling limit of Coverage A. That is how much the insurance company thinks your personal items need to be covered for. However, if the insured thinks he or she has more than the amount generated by default, the insured always can increase those limits.

Every insurance company also has determined the minimum amount that the insured's personal property should be covered for. Some insurance companies go as low as 40 percent of Coverage A. Check with your agent to be sure about the amount your personal property is insured for and to see if it is insured properly. For example, Harrison's home is insured up to $100,000. This amount is listed under Coverage A, dwelling coverage. His personal property, by default, is insured up to $60,000 because that is 60 percent of Coverage A. Harrison estimates that he doesn't have that much personal property to insure. He contacts his agent and the insurance company allows Harrison to lower personal property limits to $40,000, which is the minimum the company allows, making it 40 percent of his dwelling limit.

Personal property is covered anywhere in the world, not only on the insured's premises. For example, Beatrice is traveling to Caribbean for a vacation. She has couple of suitcases with her personal things, such as clothing, jewelry, shoes, and a video camera. If Beatrice's suitcases are damaged during the vacation or are stolen with her belongings inside, all of them are covered under her personal property coverage.

Personal property coverage is also used during a move from one location to the other. If the personal property usually is kept at the insured location, but for some reason is moved for other uses, it is covered for up to 10 percent of Coverage C. If the personal property is moved because of a move, or because of repairs being made at the residence, then the whole Coverage C limit is applied. If the insured is moving from one house to another, then personal property is covered at the full limit of Coverage C for up to thirty days.

A tenant's or boarder's personal property is not covered under this policy. Tenants should get a renter or HO-4 policy to cover his or her personal property. The insured also can add his guests or a residence employee's personal property to the policy. If the other person lives with the insured, let's say a girlfriend, but she is not the owner of the house, her boyfriend should add her personal property to his policy.

Please refer to the table below to understand how different home-owner policy forms cover personal property.

Table 2. Homeowner's Policy Coverage C (Personal Property)

Perils Insured Against	HO-1 & HO-8 forms	HO-2, HO-4 & HO-6 forms	HO-3 form	HO-5 form
Fire or Lightning	Yes	Yes	Yes	Yes
Windstorm or Hail	Yes	Yes	Yes	Yes
Explosion	Yes	Yes	Yes	Yes
Smoke	Yes	Yes	Yes	Yes
Vehicle	Yes	Yes	Yes	Yes
Aircraft	Yes	Yes	Yes	Yes
Riot or Civil Commotion	Yes	Yes	Yes	Yes
Vandalism	Yes	Yes	Yes	Yes
Theft	Yes	Yes	Yes	Yes
Volcanic Eruption	Yes	Yes	Yes	Yes
Falling Objects	No	Yes	Yes	Yes
Weight of Ice, Sleet, or Snow	No	Yes	Yes	Yes
Accidental Discharge or Overflow of Water or Stream	No	Yes	Yes	Yes
Sudden & Accidental Damage from Artificially Generated Electrical Current	No	Yes	Yes	Yes
Cracking, Bulging or Burning of Heating System, Air Conditioner, Not Water Heater	No	Yes	Yes	Yes
Freezing	No	Yes	Yes	Yes

Usually, personal property is covered on a **cash value** basis. Cash value is the amount the item can be sold for. Let's say a TV that was bought three years ago is worth less today because it was used and the value depreciated. In case of loss, the insurance company will pay the insured a replacement cost minus depreciation. Unfortunately, the cash value most of the time is not enough to buy a new item. It is very important to have your personal property insured on a **replacement cost** basis. This coverage allows you to replace damaged or lost property for how much it costs to buy a new one. Always ask your agent to add replacement cost endorsement to your personal property coverage.

Special Limits

There are personal property classes with **special limits** of coverage. Those limits can differ from policy to policy, so to be sure, please check with your agent.

Here are some examples of special limits that cover personal property:

- ▶ $200 for money or related property such as coins or precious metals, but it doesn't apply to tableware such as silverware or dishes made of gold or silver.
- ▶ $1,500 for manuscripts, securities (college thesis), and other valuable paperwork that is considered intellectual property. Papers like that are special because it took time to research them and write them. This covers the cost of replacing them.
- ▶ $1,500 for property on the residence premises used for business.
- ▶ $1,500 for property used for business that is away from premises.
- ▶ $1,500 for electronics used for business that are away from premises but are not in or around the vehicle.
- ▶ $1,500 for electronic apparatus such as CD or DVD players, iPods, iPads, and things like that, that are in the car and use the power of the car, but are normally kept in the house and are not considered vehicle equipment. A factory-installed car stereo is not covered under a homeowner's policy because it is covered under the vehicle policy.
- ▶ $1,500 for watercraft, including trailers and equipment.

▶ $1,500 for trailers on the residence premises used for business purposes.

There are special limit coverages for some things but only in a case of theft:

▶ $1,500 for jewelry, watches, furs, and precious and semiprecious stones.

▶ $1,500 for silverware, goldware, or pewterware.

▶ $2,500 for firearms.

Please check your policy or ask your agent to find out the special limits on your personal property. If you own items mentioned in these lists and think the standard coverage limit is not enough, you can add additional coverage to your policy under a **Scheduled Items Endorsement**. Property such as furs, jewelry, expensive fine art, cameras, musical instruments, golfer's equipment, silverware, coins, and stamps need to be insured properly. Your property will be itemized and added to the policy on an agreed limit. Many times insurance companies require appraisals and pictures for the items added to the scheduled items section. You should appraise your items every three to five years to ensure that they are insured properly.

Exclusions on Personal Property

Personal property should be damaged by a named peril; otherwise, it is not covered. Please refer to Table 2 for listed perils and policy forms that cover personal property. There are some circumstances where personal property will not be covered.

▶ If rain, snow, sleet, sand, or dust cause the loss, the property is not insured unless the wind or hail made an opening in the roof, broke the window, or made a way for a named peril to damage the property.

▶ Falling objects, such as trees or planes from the sky that drop on your house and damage the roof, are covered.

▶ Vehicles that go off the road, hit your home, and damage your personal property are covered under the policy.

▶ Falling objects, such as a coffee mug dropped on the floor or a mirror being unhooked from the wall and falling to the floor, are not covered.

- Theft of personal property located somewhere else that an insured rented to or occupied is not covered unless the insured is there temporarily. For example, Jenny is planning to spend her weekend at the lake house. On the way there, she stops to refuel her vehicle. While she is away from her car, her laptop is stolen. This personal property will be covered because Jenny uses the lake house as her temporarily residence.

- All kinds of animals, birds, fish, monkeys, alligators, and other animals are excluded.

- Watercraft and trailers are covered only if they are stored in an enclosed building and protected from wind and hail damage.

- If the trailer or camper and its furnishings and accessories are off the residence premises, it is not covered.

- Any motorized vehicles or aircraft, hovercraft, and their accessories and equipment are not covered and should be insured by a separate policy. A cushion vehicle or hovercraft is not covered.

- Motorized lawnmowers and motorized wheelchairs are covered only if they are used to maintain the premises or assist the handicapped insured.

- No business data, on paper, CDs, DVDs, or other storage mediums, are covered. The only items covered are prerecorded programs used in the market that you can buy, meaning you can replace them.

- Your credit cards are not covered.

- Any water that comes through your house, even if it came through your meter and you pay for the water, is not considered your property so it is not covered.

- If the personal property is damaged by a sudden and accidental tearing, burning, or cracking of heating, air conditioning system, or hot water heater or there is an accidental discharge or overflow of water or steam, the property is covered.

- If loss occurred from water or steam coming from plumbing, heating, a fire sprinkler, appliances, or an air conditioning system, it is covered.

Chapter 17

Coverage D, Loss of Use

Coverage D of a homeowner's policy pays for living expenses to the insured in case the residence is uninhabitable because of loss or damage to the residence. It covers the shortest time required to fix the damage and make the place livable again.

Loss of use coverage covers three categories: additional living expenses, fair rental value, and loss due to civil authority. The limit of this coverage is usually up to 20 percent of the dwelling amount. Although every insurance company can insure it differently, please, check with your agent to be sure about this coverage. There is no deductible on loss of use.

It includes normal every day expenses such as renting a hotel, eating at the restaurant, dry cleaners, and other justifiable, normal expenses. For example, a water pipe broke in Flint's house and destroyed the hardwood floors. While the floor is being replaced, Flint stays at the local hotel and eats at the restaurant nearby. The insurance company sees that Flint usually eats at low-price restaurants and even fast-food places, but during the house renovation, he is going for dinner to an expensive seafood restaurant. In this case, the insurance company can decline loss of use expenses. The insurance company will think Flint is taking advantage of loss of use coverage. Insurance should replace what you have, not place you better than you were.

For the insured to use this coverage, the listed perils should damage the property. If a homeowner decides to renovate his home because of a maintenance issue or decides to replace the carpet with hardwood floors, the loss of use expenses will not be covered under the insurance policy.

If the insured lives in a duplex and rents the other unit out, Coverage D covers the rents for the months that a tenant could not live in the rented property and pay the rent because of a loss and repairs.

If a civil authority prohibits an insured to live in the property because of damage by a covered peril to neighboring home, the insured's expenses are covered for a maximum of two weeks.

Chapter 18
Coverage E, Personal Liability and Coverage F, Medical Payments

All homeowner policies include liability coverage to protect the insured from financial responsibility when the insured caused property damage or personal injury to another person.

An insured can be liable for the damages incurred inside his house, such as someone falling down a staircase or slipping on a freshly mopped floor. It also covers damages outside the house, such as a in a backyard where a tree fell and dented the neighbor's car roof. An insured is responsible for his children and pets and anyone who lives under his roof.

Liability can arise not only on the premises but also outside the property. Liability coverage expands to the new property that the insured just acquired, is temporary living in, or renting as long as it is not for business use. It also covers vacant land that the insured owns or rents. Vacant land where a future residence being built and even cemetery plots or burial vaults where the insured will be eventually residing are covered.

Coverage E covers **personal liability** claims that the insured is legally obligated to pay by injuring another person or by damaging another's property. **Coverage F**, **medical payments to others**, is not legal requirements but is more of a moral obligation to the injured.

Coverage E, Personal Liability

Personal liability coverage covers the claims against an insured because he was not keeping his premises safe, was negligent, and caused damages to the other person. **Property damage** means there was physical destruction to tangible property and he or she can't use it anymore. Intangible property, such as licenses, patents, copyrights, loss of goodwill, leasehold interest, and easements are also covered.

Bodily injury means there was an injury, bodily harm, disease, sickness, or death that arises from the injury, including required care, wage loss, damage to earning capacity, medical bills, and even the inability to enjoy the activities prior to the injury. Emotional distress, such as the loss in value of savings or investments, doesn't constitute bodily injury.

Liability insurance losses are called third-party losses. Let's say your son throws a ball into your neighbor's window. You will be the first party, the insurance company is the second, and your neighbor is the third. Homeowner's policies are to insure for liability to a third party arising out of the use, occupancy, and ownership of the insured premises.

If the insured is legally obligated to pay for the bodily injury or property damage that he or she caused to the other person, the insurance company will pay the damages. More than that, the insurance company will defend the insured in lawsuits even if the charges are false. A defender will be paid until the amount reaches policy limit. Homeowner policy declarations will specify the limit of liability. There is no deductible for liability coverage. Limits can be up to $500,000, and even more if an umbrella policy is purchased in addition to existing homeowner liability limits.

Some policies also include **personal injury,** such as slander, libel, defamation, malicious prosecution, wrong eviction, false arrest, imprisonment, invasion or violation of privacy, wrongful entry, and violation of right of private occupancy. So be careful what you say about your coworkers or neighbors. If a reporter publishes the story in a local neighborhood newspaper and later it turns out to be not true, your neighbor can sue you.

Coverage F, Medical Payments to Others

Medical payments to others coverage is a low-limit coverage provided to deal with small bodily injury claims on an informal and fast basis. It doesn't matter if the insured is liable for the damage or not. Medical payment limits can be from $1,000 to $10,000 per person, per accident. This coverage will pay for medical expenses defined as reasonable charges for medical, X-ray, surgical, dental, hospital, ambulance, nursing, prosthetic devices, and even funeral expense to a person.

In order for the person to be covered, he or she should be on an insured location with the permission to be there. Covered areas also include immediate adjoining ways, such as streets, sidewalks, and roads.

The insured, the insured's pet, or a residence employee, such as gardener, housekeeper, or nanny, can do activities that caused a claim. For residence employees, an injury must happen on the homeowner's premises during employment. For example, your housekeeper hurt her back when she fell down the stars while cleaning the stairwell. That is covered. Or you give your dog to your neighbor's daughter to walk because she likes your puppy so much, but your dog bites another kid in a leg. Let say your kids were playing in the backyard with neighborhood kids and one of them got a cut on broken glass. The fast medical attention expenses are covered.

Payments to others usually can be covered if the claim was filed up to a three years after the occurrence.

Additional Coverage

Additional coverage is included in a homeowner policy without an additional premium in addition to existing limits of liability. An insurance company will pay only up to a policy limit. It can be a little bit different from one policy to the other, but overall additional coverage includes claims expense, first aid to others, property damage of others, and loss assessment.

▶ The insurance company covers **claims expenses**. The expenses that the insurer incurs, such as jury and filing fees, cost of service, witness and attorney's fees, deposition costs, fees for transcripts of court proceedings, photocopying costs, reasonable bond premiums that were required in suits that the insured appeals, premium for bonds and bail bond, and other kinds of bonds.

▶ Reasonable expenses are covered when an insured incurred the expenses at the insurance company's request, such as up to $250 a day in lost earnings when an insured was assisting the insurance company's hired defense counsel to investigate or defend a suit and post judgment or the portion of the judgment that was paid in court. Prejudgment interest is also included in the liability coverage. It is used when a court rewards a third party for a compensation that could have been paid before the actual judgment was pronounced.

▶ **First aid expense** covers the expense of first aid to others the insured incurred. Expenses related to the immediate medical attention right after the other person injures himself are covered. This coverage has no limit, because the first aid to others provides good will. Example, Cherry's friend comes for dinner. Cherry's kitchen floor is freshly mopped, and her friend slips on it and falls. The friend rushes to the emergency for stitches. Cherry's policy will pay the medical expense of $350.

▶ **Damage to the property of others** covers for damages that the insured caused to the other person's property. Usually, property that is in the care, custody, or control of the insured is not covered under a homeowner's policy. But if the additional coverage is added, the property that is physically damaged can be covered up to $1,000. If the insured intentionally damages something, the insured owns the property, or a tenant living in the insured's house owns the property, the damage is not covered.

▶ **Loss assessment** coverage pays up to $1,000 for the insured's share of the homeowner's or condominium association to cover liability loss. Endorsement to the policy might add higher limits of the coverage.

Exclusions

The **exclusion of liability** policies include damage to the property of an insured or to the property in the insured's care, bodily injury to the insured or his family members, and losses covered under workers' compensation.

The insurance company will not cover expected or intended losses because they are not fortuitous.

The following items are excluded.

▶ Any insured who intentionally causes property or bodily damage to another is not covered. Moreover, saying, "I did not mean it" will not help.

▶ The insurance company will cover reasonable force needed to protect yourself or another person and their property, but only if the defense was necessary. Losses will be covered when dealing with property crime, such as theft, burglary, or arson.

▶ An insured can use lethal force only when forced to use it to protect himself or others because he or she is being threatened by lethal force. If you use the force in response to a threat that exceeds the permissible level, you will be the one called the aggressor. From a legal standpoint, you will the one who is assaulting, not the one who is defending. Insurance companies advise keeping it cool in situations like that. Do not escalate the confrontation, and do not gather a group of friends to take care of the matter. Going over the line, even if it is a close call, can easily jeopardize your right to insurance coverage. If you are the subject of criminal prosecution, the insurance company can deny defense counsel in your criminal case and deny paying a resulting judgment against you.

▶ Communicable diseases, such as sexually transmitted diseases, are also not covered. Any kind abuse that can be mental or physical, corporal punishment, or sexual molestation is also excluded.

▶ Any losses that occur by using, selling, manufacturing, delivering, transferring, or possessing controlled substances, such as drugs, are excluded from the coverage.

► If the insured damages the property of another or injures another person while under the influence of a controlled substance, the insurance company will not cover any damage.

► More than that, if an insured furnishes controlled substances to a third party who is then injured while being under the influence, coverage would be excluded for any personal property damage or injury suit against the insured.

► If the insured has an illegal drug lab that catches on fire and damages adjoining properties, any resulting lawsuit against the insured will not be covered. Overall, if there is any loss that includes controlled substances, none of them will be covered.

► Any losses for any personal property damage or injury caused directly by war, rebellion, insurrection, or terrorism are not covered. Anything associated with nuclear reaction, radioactive contamination, or consequential injuries is excluded.

► There are exclusions for rental property. Liability coverage precludes coverage for any property damage to the property that the insured rented, occupied, used, or had in his care. A rental property is covered only for property damages such as fire, smoke, or explosion.

► Coverage also excludes losses incurred by ownership, maintenance, operation, occupancy, loading, unloading of watercraft, aircraft, hovercraft, or other motor vehicles. All mentioned vehicles should have a separate insurance policy.

Vehicles, Watercraft, and Planes

Vehicles are not covered if used in any prearranged or organized race, speed contest, or other competition. Golf cars are only covered when used on the golf facility. There is no coverage if a vehicle is used for business purposes, used to carry persons or cargo, or rented to somebody.

However, a motor vehicle is covered if it is in storage on an insured location or used to service an insured's residence, such as lawn mower. Motor vehicles that assist the handicapped are also covered under the policy. Motor vehicles, owned or not owned by the insured but used for recreational use off public roads or on the insured's location, are also covered.

The homeowner's policy does not cover watercraft if it is used for business purposes or is raced, rented to others, or carrying cargo.

The watercraft is covered if it is stored in the closed building at the insured's location. If the sailing vessel is less than twenty-six feet long, it is covered if the insured owns, rents, or borrows it. Outboard watercraft less than twenty-five horsepower are covered if the insured owns, rents, or borrows it. If the watercraft is powered by an inboard or inboard/out-drives of fifty horsepower or less, it is covered if it is rented or borrowed. If the insured owns it, then it is not covered and needs to be insured by separate watercraft policy. For more information, please read Chapter 35.

If you own a private plane and a friend injures his finger when the insured closes the door on it, it is not covered because the damage arises from owning an aircraft. Property that the insured owns, uses, rents, or borrows is not covered.

Residence Employees

Bodily injury losses to any person who is eligible to receive benefits under workers' compensation laws, nonoccupational disability, or occupational disease laws are not covered. Residence employees, such as housekeepers, nannies, and gardeners, can be insured with an endorsement.

If a residence employee suffers bodily injury at an insured location, any medical payment will be covered even if the injury did not occur within the course of employment. If bodily injury occurred off premises but within the course of employment and is caused by employment, medical payments will be covered.

Business Ownership

Another area of exclusion is **business ownership**. Homeowner's policies do not cover losses incurred by business ownership. It can be added as an endorsement to the policy, depending on the insurance company.

Definition of business ownership means a profession, trade, or occupation that engages in an occasional, part-time, full-time basis, or any activity that is engaged in to make money or other compensation. A person can be insured by the policy if he received less than $2,000 in total compensation within a twelve-month period prior to the effective day of the policy. Volunteer activities with no compensation received, except for reimbursements of expenses, are not considered a business. Home day care service provided to a relative is not considered a business.

The exceptions to business exclusions include renting part of the residence premises or portions, such as a garage, to use as an office, school, or studio. If the insured is under the age of twenty-one and is involved in an occasional, self-employed business, by himself or herself, this exclusion will not apply. For example, your son is being paid for mowing lawns and raking leaves on the weekend for your neighbors. That will not be considered a business. Your daughter babysitting for pay also won't be a business. But an insured attorney who meets with clients in his home and is later sued for giving erroneous advice is not covered because he was rendering professional services and should have had a separate professional liability policy.

There are more exclusions unique to every policy, so please check with your agent.

Chapter 19
Additional Coverage

There are coverages included in a standard homeowner's policy at no additional cost to the insured, but depending on the policy, these coverages can have some limitations. The following items are **additional coverages**.

▶ Reasonable repairs to the damaged property to protect it from more damage are covered, as are the materials the insured had to buy to protect the property from additional damage. For example, Oscar buys a couple of sheets of plywood to cover a broken window to protect the room against the rain. The insurance company will reimburse his expenses.

▶ Additions, alterations, or other improvements done at the insured's expense. Tenant's policy, Form 4, covers up to 10 percent of the Coverage C, personal property limit. For example, Nelly, with property owner content, updates the kitchen cabinets in the house she rents. This improvement will be covered.

▶ Property removed from a damaged home is covered when it is stored in another location while the house is rebuilt or repaired. This covers the property against a direct loss from any peril while it is being removed from the damaged premises. The property that is removed from the main residence is covered up to thirty days. For example, Kristina's carpet was stolen while it was being stored at another place while her home was being rebuilt after the fire. Kristina will be reimbursed for her carpet.

▶ Reasonable expenses for debris removal, such as:
  * Tree limbs from the insured's or a neighbor's trees
  * Trees hit by lightning
  * Property damaged by fire or explosion
  * Damage from a vehicle or aircraft not operated by the insured
  * Ashes or other particles of volcanic eruption
  * A riot, vandalism, or malicious mischief
  * Theft

▶ Trees, bushes, shrubs, or lawns and plants are covered if they fall on the structure or are blocking a driveway or ramp for the handicapped. The loss should be caused by a fire, lightning, explosion, vehicle, aircraft, riot or civil commotion, vandalism or malicious mischief, or theft. Coverage to damaged trees is up to 5 percent of the dwelling coverage, but it can't be more that $500 for one tree or $1,000 per occurrence. A tenant's policy has this coverage also. It is 20 percent of Coverage C. A unit owner's policy covers trees and shrubs up to 10 percent of Coverage C. To be sure of the limit, please contact your agent.

▶ A fire department service charge, such as charges incurred when the fire department is called to the property, is covered to $500.

▶ If fire destroyed the insured property, the insurance company even can pay for information about the arson that caused the fire, although there is a limit for how much the insurance company is willing to pay per person and per event.

▶ A house collapse because of defective materials or methods in construction is covered. It is also covered if the collapse is caused by named perils on the policy or by the decay or insects and vermin damage hidden from the plain view and not known to the insured.

All forms cover the collapse when it is caused by the weight of people, contents, equipment, or rain that collects on the roof.

► Glass or safety glazing material that is damaged, such as that on storm doors and windows or glass that is part of the building.

► Credit cards, fund transfer cards, and counterfeit money that the insured accepted in good faith are covered. Forgery is covered up to $500 for theft or unauthorized use of funds by forgery or alteration of the insured's checks.

► Loss assessment covers an assessment by your homeowner's association or condo owner's association for damages up to the limits listed on your policy. Damages include a direct loss to the property owned by everyone in the subdivision or neighborhood, such as a clubhouse, common fountains, flowerbeds, children's playground, and common pools. No matter how many assessments were done, only one deductible can be applied. Loss assessment additional coverage provides up to $1,000 or more, depending on the policy for the named insured's share of a loss assessment charged against the insured by the homeowner's association, cooperative association, or condominium. Coverage applies when the assessment includes covered bodily injury, liability, or property damage to a trustee, director, or an officer while on such duty. Regardless of the number of assessments imposed, a $1,000 limit applies to all accidents covering a board member. This coverage excludes an assessment charged by any government body. For example, if the city imposes an assessment for street repair and repaving, no coverage exists to cover this provision.

► All forms cover ordinance of law. This coverage pays up to 10 percent of the Coverage A limit to rebuild or improve the dwelling with other structures to become compliant with applicable building and land use codes.

► Landlord's furnishings coverage covers up to $2,500 for loss to the furnishings, such as loss of appliances, carpeting, faucets, or furniture in the apartment, room, or home that is rented out, in

Forms 2, 3, and 5. It does not cover a tenant's or unit owner's personal property.

► Grave markers and mausoleums in the cemetery are covered up to $5,000 for damage, if a covered peril causes the damage.

Every insurance company has different additional coverages listed on the policy. Please read your policy or contact your agent to obtain more information.

Chapter 20

Form HO-4, Tenant's (Renter's) Coverage

I f you watch the news occasionally, you probably have seen a breaking news report about an apartment building that burned to the ground. Most of the time when fire strikes, it damages a couple of apartment units, leaving the tenants with nothing. I am sure you have also noticed the interviews with the local residents who are crying because "all they had" was burned, and they have no idea how they will replenish their belongings. Many of them did not carry **tenant's policy** HO-4, which is also called renter's insurance. If you are renting an apartment, a house, a townhouse, or any other space, please insure your personal belongings and prevent financial hardship from loss.

Tenant's Policy Coverage

There is not much difference between a tenant's policy and a homeowner's policy. The only difference is that a tenant's policy does not cover the actual building where the tenant is living. As with any other policy, a tenant policy covers against perils such as:

- ► Fire
- ► Lightning

- ► Windstorm
- ► Hail
- ► Hurricane
- ► Explosion
- ► Smoke
- ► Aircraft
- ► Vehicle
- ► Riot or civil commotion
- ► Malicious mischief
- ► Theft
- ► Falling objects
- ► Volcanic eruption
- ► Weight of ice, sleet, or snow
- ► Freezing
- ► Cracking and accidental discharge of water from a hot water heater or air conditioner
- ► Any damage generated from electrical current.
- ► Fungi, wet or dry rot, and bacteria coverage can be added by an endorsement or is automatically built into your policy. Check with your insurance provider.

Following is an explanation of the different types of coverage that you might find in your tenant's policy.

Coverage C, Personal Property

This coverage is similar to a homeowner's HO-3 policy. Every insurance company has its own coverage limits, usually starting at $25,000. If you think your personal property is worth more, you should definitely insure it for more. Although coverage is provided only on an actual cash value basis, replacement cost coverage can be added as an endorsement. It might sound like it is not a big deal to have your personal things insured with actual cash value, but it makes a big difference when your couch was burned and now you need to buy a new one.

Actual cash value is calculated by taking the replacement cost of the new item and depreciating it over time. For example, the leather couch that Celina bough five years ago was worth $4,000. That is much more than the insurance company is willing to pay Celina using an actual cash value basis. The insurance company has a depreciation calculator and decides that paying Celina $850 is enough. If she has a full value personal property endorsement on her policy and can prove that she paid $4,000 for the couch, the insurance company will replace the couch. It probably won't be the same couch, but it will be enough money to buy new one. For a couple of dollars more a year, this additional coverage is worth having. Make sure your agent adds this endorsement on your tenant's policy.

Depending on the insurance company, some personal property is not eligible for replacement cost, such as antiques, fine arts, paintings, memorabilia, collector's items, and souvenirs. Overall, any obsolete items should be added on the policy as scheduled items endorsement. For more information, please read Chapter 8. Any personal property items not owned by the insured, not used, or in poor condition are not covered. The insurance company will repair damaged items or replace it for you, whichever costs less. For any questions about how to submit or handle the claim, please refer to the homeowner's claims section in Chapter 24.

When a decorating show inspires you to update the look of the apartment or room that you rent, contact your landlord to ask for permission. If he or she agrees to updates to the place, you can replace the light fixtures, update the kitchen, or improve the bathroom's appearance. Usually the insurance policy does not cover improvements of the tenant makes at the tenant's expense, but these can be covered by an endorsement. Additional coverage can be obtained up to 10 percent of Coverage C or even higher if requested. If the tenant has a waterbed, the landlord can require the tenant to have insurance to cover the damage that the bed can cause, especially if the rented space is on the second floor or higher.

When you are moving between apartments or houses, your personal property is insured up to 25 percent or even 100 percent of Coverage C. Please contact your agent to know the actual amount that you are covered. Items left in the car and stolen are also covered under personal property coverage, subject to a deductible.

Coverage D, Additional Living Expense and Loss of Rent

Coverage D covers up to 20 percent of Coverage C. It covers the expenses that might occur from the rental space being uninhabitable due to damage by covered perils mentioned earlier. Expenses covered include hotel or food expenses to keep normal standard of living. For example, the apartment that Nancy rents experienced water damage. While her apartment is being renovated, she needs to stay at the hotel and eat at the restaurant. The insurance company will reimburse those kinds of expenses. Remember, those expenses should be considered normal, everyday expenses, not an extravagant vacation. Don't be surprised when the insurance company declines to pay for your dinner at Red Lobster and a five-star hotel when you usually eat at a Jack in the Box and are staying at La Quinta. For more details, see your policy or contact your agent with questions.

Coverage E, Personal Liability

This covers bodily injury and property damage that the insured is liable for to the other person. A tenant's policy liability losses definition is the same as a homeowner's policy for Coverage E. The minimum limit usually starts as low as $25,000 each occurrence and can go as high as $500,000, depending on the insurance company writing the policy. For example, Barbara has a tenant policy with a $100,000 liability limit. After moving in, she is having a get-together party at her rental, which is a two-story townhouse. A guest trips on the staircase, hurts her knee, and sues Barbara for negligence. If Barbara is liable for the bodily injury, the insurance company will pay for the legal fees and other expenses up to the coverage limits, which is up to $100,000 in this case.

Coverage F, Medical Payments

This covers payments made to others. The limit per person can start at $250 and go as high as $10,000, depending on the insurance company coverage options. Medical payment coverage includes visits to the emergency room, small medical bills, X-rays, prosthetic devices, dental services, hospital stays, and more. For example, Sofia's tenant policy carries $1,000 medical payments to others coverage limit. One weekend, she is having a graduation party and asks her sister to help her with a salad. Her sister accidentally cuts her finger and is rushed to the emergency room for stitches. Sofia's sister's expenses will be covered by the tenant's policy, up to $1,000.

The policy will not cover bodily injury or personal property loss to the person who is on the insured's premises without a permission or who does the damage to himself or his or her property on purpose. The policy also does not cover damage that arises out of a violation of criminal law or damage that is committed with the knowledge or consent of the insured.

Depending on the insurance company, other coverage or endorsement options can be available to you. For more information, ask your agent.

Premium Payments

A tenant's policy, just like a homeowner's policy, is usually issued for a year. You can cancel your policy any time you want. The part of the premium being applied for the future coverage will be refunded to you. When your tenant's policy is issued, you should choose the premium payment option. You can pay your policy annually, quarterly, or monthly. If you chose to receive the bill by mail, don't be surprised that for every bill you get in the mail, you are charged an additional $2 to $5. It is good idea to set your monthly payments to be deducted automatically from your account to save on processing fees. The insurance company has no right to deduct a larger amount from your account. If you make any changes to your policy, it takes usually thirty days for the change to affect your bill.

If the insurance company changes anything on your policy, you will be notified by mail first, before the payment is deducted from your account. Just make sure that when you change your credit card you notify the insurance company, so the next payment will be taken from your account. Any changes with your credit card, depending on the insurance company, can take a week or a whole month for the changes to take effect. Plan accordingly. For more information about premium payment options, ask your agent.

Chapter 21

Form HO-6, Unit Owner's (Condo) Coverage

The unit owner's policy is very similar to the homeowner's and provides coverage mostly to condominium and townhouse owners. Structures as that is an individual housing unit that shares other common structure elements, such as common walls, sidewalks, hallways, recreational facilities, and pools with other unit owners.

Unit owners should read and keep the copy of the condominium association's insurance policy to understand what it covers. Every condominium has different insurance coverage depending on the level of ownership. Declarations of ownership specify what the unit owner owns and how much insurance he or she needs to purchase. Ownership of the unit can be broad, just the bare walls, or anything in between.

The **broad form concept** includes building items, such as wall coverings, appliances, and lighting fixtures, as part of the building. The condominium association's commercial insurance policy covers these items. In this case, the owner of the unit should purchase insurance that covers the items not covered under that policy.

The **bare walls** concept specifies all the building items the unit owner is responsible for and needs to be insured against in addition to the condominium association's insurance policy. It may cover wall coverings, kitchen bathroom fixtures, lighting fixtures, carpeting, and other property within the condominium or townhouse unit.

The following coverage items are used in a unit owner's policy:

- ▶ **Coverage A, Dwelling** is usually low because of the building items the condominium association's insurance policy covers. Dwelling coverage includes appliances, cabinets, and improvements that are part of the owner's unit, as well as exterior items that are part of the residence, such as windows and patio doors. Coverage A also covers any common area that the unit owner is responsible for and any buildings that aren't attached to the unit, such as a garage. Dwelling coverage is usually insured for actual cash value but can be endorsed with replacement cost. You should check with your association to see if you need to provide coverage for any other areas.

- ▶ **Coverage C, Personal Property** covers the same personal items as Coverage C for a homeowner's policy, such as clothing, furniture, and other items the insured purchased. The limit on this coverage is selected based on the value of the possessions rather than simply calculating it as a percentage of Coverage A. Coverage is provided on an actual cash value basis, but replacement cost coverage may be available.

- ▶ **Coverage D, Loss of Use** coverage is the same as the homeowner's policy except that the limit is 40 percent of Coverage C. It covers the unit owner's expenses, such as meals and hotel, if the unit is unavailable, such as when repairs are being done to the unit when it is damaged.

Liability Coverage

There are two types of liability coverage: personal liability and medical payments to others. It is the same on all forms of homeowner's policies, including the tenant's form.

Personal Liability covers injury and damage to property that the insured is legally responsible for. For example, the dog bites a passerby, a neighbor is injured in your swimming pool, or your bathtub overflows into the apartment or unit below. The usual limit for this coverage is $100,000, but higher limits may be purchased. This section also covers your acts away from your home in the event you injure someone while golfing or hunting, for example.

Medical payments coverage will pay for medical bills, doctor visits, X-rays, and other medical expenses to other people due to the injuries the insured caused. The insured can choose medical payment limits as low as $500 or as high as $10,000.

Please check with your insurance agent to be sure you know what your policy covers. Make sure there are no insurance gaps between your personal policy and the condominium association's insurance policy.

Chapter 22
Mobile Homes

Mobile homes are excluded by homeowner's policies, although they have many similar characteristics as a home. Because mobile homes are more fragile, they are more likely to be exposed to wind and fire damage, involved in a collision, or upset while transported, and insurance companies don't like to insure them.

A mobile home can be insured by a separate mobile home policy or, depending on the insurance provider, can be added by an endorsement to the homeowner's policy. A specific mobile home package policy can be added to HO-2 or HO-3 form to modify the coverage for mobile homeowners.

Mobile homes permanently placed on a foundation can be insured by the dwelling policy basic form, DP-1. A tenant's form can be used to cover the contents and personal property of a mobile home.

Any equipment and accessories originally built into the unit are covered. Other structures located on the premises but detached from the mobile home are covered up to 10 percent of the mobile home's value.

The liability section for this coverage is similar to a homeowner's policy and covers against bodily injury and property damage to the other person done by the insured. The policy also covers additional living expenses while the mobile home is unlivable and in the process of repair. Damage to the mobile home from collision or upset while it is transit is available as an optional coverage.

Mobile homes can be insured with replacement cost or actual cash value. Replacement cost will replace your mobile home in case of total loss. Actual cash value will insure its depreciated value. If possible, add replacement cost endorsements on the dwelling and your personal property items to be fully covered.

Chapter 23

Perils

An insurance policy covers a property against covered causes of loss listed on the policy. Loss can be direct, such as the house was destroyed by fire, or indirect, such as living expenses while the damaged property is repaired.

Every policy form and insurance policy, depending on the insurance company, covers against different **perils**. Some perils are common to all forms, while other perils are not.

Basic Named Perils

Homeowner's insurance covers basic named perils. These perils include fire, lightning, windstorm, hail, explosions, smoke, volcanic eruption, impact by vehicles and aircraft, theft, riot, civil commotion, and vandalism and malicious mischief. If a windstorm or hail makes an opening in the dwelling structure, such a broken window or torn roof, and thus damages the interior of the house, such damage is covered. Smoke, soot, fumes from a furnace, or vapor from a boiler or similar equipment is covered. Smoke from fireplaces, agricultural smudging, or industrial operations are not covered under this form.

The portion of the property rented out to a tenant is not covered. Tenant belongings should be covered under renter's insurance, and the tenant is responsible to obtain it.

Theft, even attempted theft, is covered. However, it doesn't cover theft by the insured. Mysterious disappearance of jewelry or other expensive items belonging to the insured are not covered. If you went to the movies and had a diamond ring, and you noticed the ring was not on your finger when you went back home, the standard basic peril policy won't cover the loss. These items can be covered by scheduling the items on your homeowner's policy with a special endorsement. See Chapter 16, Coverage C.

If the property was vacant for more than sixty consecutive days, vandalism or malicious mischief is not covered. If the dwelling is under construction and nobody lives in the house, the losses that might occur will not be covered unless you are insured under a builder's risk policy, which is separate from a homeowner's policy.

Broad Named Perils

In addition to basic perils, broad named perils add more coverage. Examples are below.

- ► Falling objects are covered, but only if the object makes an opening in a roof or wall before damaging the personal property or interiors.
- ► Weight of ice, snow, or sleet is covered, but it doesn't cover the weight causing damage to awnings, fences, patios, swimming pools, foundations, pavements, bulkheads, wharves, docks, or piers.
- ► Accidental discharge of water or steam from appliances or plumbing or related systems are covered, but it does not include discharge or overflow of water from a sump pump.
- ► It will cover sudden and accidental rupture of a heating unit, air conditioner, water heating system, or fire sprinkler.
- ► Freezing of plumbing or other related systems is covered unless the house is unoccupied. An unoccupied house is not covered.

Losses will be covered if the homeowner took care of the building by draining the water from the systems, shut off the supply, and kept the heating on.

▶ Fireplace smoke is covered under broad coverage form.

▶ Damage made by a vehicle to a fence, driveway, or walk while vehicle is owned or operated by a person who lives in the insured household.

Special Form Coverage

Special form coverage provides all risk coverage to the dwelling and other structures listed on the policy. There are two differences between all risk coverage and a named perils coverage. **All risk coverage** or open peril covers direct physical loss incurred to a covered property, unless the damage cause was excluded. **Named perils coverage** covers the loss to a property only if the loss is caused by a peril that was specifically listed on the policy. An all risk policy covers more than named perils policy.

If the loss is caused by the water damage from a household appliance, protective fire sprinkler system, air conditioning system, plumbing, or heating and is not excluded from covered perils, then the cost of tearing the walls and repairing or replacing them is covered. It doesn't cover actual plumbing or system repairs. It only covers repairs to the walls or floor—the structural losses.

Exclusions

Although policies cover many causes of loss, there are exclusions to the policy.

▶ All homeowner forms exclude water damage, such as from flooding or overflow from a sump pump, although sump pump coverage can be added to the policy as an endorsement. To find out more about flood insurance, please go to Chapter 36.

▶ Losses caused by **earth movement**, such as earthquake, mine subsidence, and landslides, are not covered. However, the coverage can be purchased separately as an addition to the policy or as a standalone policy. This type of coverage can be purchased only in areas prone to those kinds of losses. So let's say you live in Texas. You can't purchase earthquake coverage, because there are no earthquakes in Texas. Aftershocks that occur within seventy-two hours of the original quake constitute a single earthquake. This policy covers building and personal property damaged or lost in the earthquake.

▶ **Power interruptions** that take place outside the property are not covered. Food spoilage is not covered when it is caused by power outages, but this can be added to your policy by an endorsement.

▶ Any losses from war or nuclear hazard are not covered.

▶ **Ordinance of Law** is an important area of coverage. If your house needs to be rebuilt according to current ordinances and codes, your regular policy will not cover this extra cost without this coverage added to the policy. The enforcement of any builder's law relating to the repair, demolition, or construction of a property is not covered, although it can be added as an endorsement.

▶ There is no coverage if the insured intentionally damages the property or if the insured does not preserve the property after the loss to protect it from additional damage.

▶ **Seizure of the Property** by a public authority or government, or destruction or confiscation caused by the government is not covered. For example, if a governmental body acts to prevent a fire from spreading and damages your property, the loss will be covered. But if the government seizes the property based on an arrest or conviction for crimes and offenses, the losses will not be covered.

▶ **Collapse** of your house is not covered unless the loss is covered under the policy or added as an additional coverage to the policy.

▶ **Maintenance** of the property is not covered. Poor design, building site, materials, or construction are not covered. Defective planning, zoning, surveying, development, and siting are not covered. The insured is responsible for making sure the property is well maintained. It is important to inspect the property before buying it. The insured is responsible for making sure that the contractors who are remodeling, repairing, renovating, or reconstructing the property are competent to perform such updates and are licensed and insured companies and individuals. None of the do-it-yourself remodeling or construction projects that cause a loss is covered, and there is no coverage due to defective, faulty, or inadequate materials, specifications, or design.

► Loss caused by **vermin, birds, insects, or animals** the insured owns are also not covered.

► **Wear and tear,** deterioration, inherent vice, mechanical break-down, rust, smog, corrosion, wet or dry rot, smoke from agricultural smudging, or industrial operations, and anything that can be considered an expected losses that comes with using something over an extended time is not covered. Also not covered is settling, bulging, expansion, shrinking, or foundation, floors, walls, roof, pavement, or ceiling cracking.

► **Freezing** of plumbing, air conditioning, or heating systems damage is excluded while the property was vacant, unoccupied, or under construction, and the systems were not maintained well.

► **Foundations, retaining walls, or nonbuilding structures such as fences, swimming pools, and docks** are not covered from damages caused by freezing; pressure or weight of water, ice, or snow; and thawing of snow or ice. Damages caused by drought, such as damage to a foundation, are also not covered. Those losses are considered maintenance issues that are the insured's responsibility.

► **A Dwelling under construction and materials used for construction** are not covered for loss such as theft. For this kind of loss, a builder's risk policy should be purchased.

► **Fungi, wet rot, and mold** are not covered if caused by a sump pump, related equipment, or a roof drain, downspout, or gutter. None of the repeated seepage or leakage of water is covered.

Please check with your agent to comprehend exactly what your policy covers and excludes.

Chapter 24
Submit a Claim

To **submit a claim**, you can call the insurance company directly or you can call your agent first. If you have a good agent, he or she will tell you what claims you should submit to the insurance company and which ones you should not. Many think, "That is why I have insurance. They should pay for it!" That is true, but small claims hurt you in a long run. Any claim, big or small, goes on your record and influences your renewal with the same company or even quoting with other company. Insurance companies share claims information with each other.

Several sections on your policy affect how claims are paid.

► **Limit of Liability** is the limit for one occurrence shown on the declarations page, regardless of how many claims have been made already. The coverage applies to each insured separately.

► The **Loss Settlement** section of your policy it describes how a claim payment will be paid. The payment is always made to the named insured on the policy, unless some other person is legally entitled to receive a payment and steps forward. The losses to the property should be paid in actual cash or replacement cost value and can't be more than the amount necessary to pay for the repairs.

▶ The **deductible clause** states that the amount minus deductible will be paid to the insured for the losses. The **pair of set** states that the insurance company doesn't have to pay for the whole set, only for repair of a part, or replacement of a piece, but not the whole set.

▶ The **recovered property** clause states that if the insured has been paid for the loss and then recovers it, he or she needs to notify the insurance company and give back the loss settlement.

After the insured makes the loss statement, losses should be paid in a "reasonable time," and both the insurer and the insured agree to the amount of loss. The insurance company has thirty days to give a check to the insured to make proper repairs or replace damaged property. Different insurance companies have different processing times. If there is a catastrophic loss in your area, it is likely that your claim will not be handled faster than during the times the insurance company is not as busy.

After the claim is made, and the adjuster makes a decision, the insurance company will send the check for the lost property or repairs. When there is a dispute between the insurance company and the insured about the value of the property, either can request an appraisal of the property to be made and presented to resolve the disputes. Each party selects the appraiser within twenty days of the notice and selects an umpire. Each appraiser appraises the loss separately and presents their findings to the umpire. If within fifteen days neither party can agree on the umpire, the judge of the district court where the loss occurred will select the umpire. The agreement is binding to both parties. Any costs and fees of the umpire are split between two parties.

There is more than one way to calculate the loss.

▶ **Actual cash value** is calculated by replacement cost minus depreciation. Actual cash value insures the old property that exhibits signs of wear and tear.

▶ **Replacement cost** is the cost to replace damaged property with the like kind and the quality without taking in consideration the depreciation. For example, Aida has replacement cost on her personal property. After the fire in the kitchen damages her breakfast table with chairs, Aida submits a claim. Because her policy indicated replacement cost on her personal property, she will receive a check from the insurance company to replace her destroyed breakfast set, and it will be enough money to go and buy a new set. If she were insured up to actual cash value, she would receive a smaller check, because the insurance company would calculate the depreciation for those three years that Aida had the set. An endorsement can add replacement cost value.

► A **functional replacement cost** is also used as an alternative form to evaluate the damaged property. With this coverage, the insured can replace the damaged property with something that suits the insured better at the given situation. Let say Daniel has an old shack built fifty years ago. Originally, it was built of wood, but now, after the fire destroyed the shack, Daniel wants to replace it with metal. Insurance policy limits can be lower on the policy, since Daniel will not be rebuilding the same wooded shack. He won't be replacing original building.

► **Market value** is the amount of money the insured can get by selling the property to another person. Insurance has nothing to do with market value. The dwelling limit on the policy is the amount of money that insurance will pay to rebuild the home. For auto policies, market value or blue book value have an impact determining the amount paid to the insured after the total loss.

► **Agreed value** is the amount of insurance carried on a particular item, where the insurance company and the insured came into agreement about the amount.

► **Stated amount** is a method where the item is insured up to the maximum amount payable indicated in the policy. This type of method is mostly used for autos and boats.

► **Valued policy** is used for scheduled items appraised by certified appraisers and is listed on the policy. Any valuable pieces of art, expensive furs, or jewelry would fall into this category.

When a Claim Is Declined

Your homeowner's claim can be declined if you have a homeowner's policy and the property you own is not occupied or is rented out. A vacant house means nobody lives there and there is no personal property in it. Many insurance companies don't want to deal with rented or vacant properties because of the heightened risk of loss and liability.

If you are not happy about how a claim is handled, you can file a **suit against the insurer.** Just remember that the action against the insurance company can be brought only if the insured followed all policy terms and conditions. Also, there is a limited time to sue, usually within two years after the date of loss. You can find more information about that in your policy.

Your Claim and the Lawsuit

If your claim ends up in a **lawsuit**, it is important to try promptly forward any legal documents that the insurance company asks you to submit and to give permission to make copies of those documents. If there is a trial, provide your sworn statement about the event and attend all hearings and examinations.

Different states have different laws about how the examinations should be done and when they are really needed. Such examinations should be conducted with reasonable notice, time, and at a convenient place. The insurance company does not always require examinations under oath. They are only requested in cases where the insurer found the insured to be uncooperative with the investigation or if there is something that indicates the case is fraudulent. Refusal to submit an examination under the oath allows the insurance company to decline the claim all together.

The examination is done before a court reporter, usually a lawyer the insurance company appoints. The court reporter writes down the insured's answers to the questions. The insured can have counsel present at the time of examination to assert any objection to a questions asked. After the examination is done, the insurer should provide a free copy of the transcript of the examination. The insured can make sworn corrections to the transcript if desired.

Part V

Insuring What You Drive

Introduction

Personal auto insurance is the most popular insurance, and the majority of insurance claims filed every year are auto insurance claims. No matter how good of a driver you are, it is possible to end up in an accident that is somebody else's fault. It is important to have a personal auto policy that will cover not only the other driver in the accident, but also your own vehicle and passengers in case the driver at fault has no insurance.

Chapter 25
How Auto Policy Premiums Are Determined

Auto policy premiums are determined in a similar way to home-owner's or dwelling policy premiums. Understanding what factors work in your favor or against you will help you make better decisions in purchasing a personal auto insurance policy. Here are some factors that the insurance company takes into an account when determining your rate. To be more precise, check with your insurance agent, because ratings can differ from one company to the other.

1. **Amount of coverage**. A personal auto policy consists of a couple of kinds of coverage that can be purchased separately or together. Every auto insurance policy has **liability coverage** with limits to cover other person's bodily injury or property damage. This coverage is applied per person and per accident. The policy also covers your vehicle property damage and bodily injury expenses in case the other party is at fault and their insurance company cannot pay for the losses. Although the insurance company cannot require you to carry higher coverage limits than state law requires, the higher the limits you carry, the better. If you have

an automobile loan, your lender will require you to have **collision and comprehensive coverage** to pay for any damages to your vehicle. Other coverage found in the auto policy includes **medical payments** or **personal injury protection** to pay for the medical bills and expenses due to the accident. **Towing and labor** and **roadside assistance** are other useful coverage to have. The more coverage you have, the higher the premium.

2. **Amount of the deductible**. A deductible is the portion of the claim that you must pay before the insurance company will cover the rest of the claim. Just like with other policies, the higher the deductible, the lower the premium. Before choosing a high deductible to keep your premium low, make sure you have enough money to pay it in case of an accident. The deductible for collision and comprehensive losses can be as low as $250 and high as $2,000, depending on the amount you choose. If you are still paying for the vehicle, your lienholder will let you know how high your deductible can be. Usually, it is no more than $1,000.

3. **Location.** Where your car is garaged is also very important. Every zip code has its own rate. An insurance company likes to do business in some areas and avoids others. The insurance company keeps statistical data to determine how profitable it is to do business in that particular area. Depending on how profitable the area is, the insurance company can choose to insure more drivers or stop servicing the area all together. Neighborhoods in flood zones, common hurricane areas, or areas where natural disasters are common are not that welcome. Even the same city can have multiple areas with different rates. Residents of neighborhoods with higher numbers of accidents, traffic violations, hit-and-run incidents, stolen vehicles, and break-ins pay higher rates.

4. **Personal profile and credit score**. Depending on your personal profile, your insurance rates can be high or low. Some insurance companies like to do business with students in their twenties; some companies like more mature clients. Every driver's age on

the policy makes a difference. Boys under twenty-five and girls under twenty-one will receive higher rates because they are statistically proven to be more prone to accidents and traffic violations. There are companies who give a discount to drivers more than fifty-five years old. Your marital status also makes a difference. Insurance companies like married drivers, counting them as more responsible than singles. If you are a homeowner, you will receive a better rate than someone who is renting or who lives with his or her parents. Insurance companies also like employed individuals with a high level of education, as they are better at paying bills on time. Your credit score is also a big factor in determining your premium rates. The higher the credit score, the lower the insurance premium. When the insurance company checks your credit score, it is considered a "soft hit" for insurance proposes and makes no difference to your score.

5. **Claims history.** No insurance company likes to insure a driver with violations or many claims. It is normal for a driver to have one or two tickets or a claim here or there. Some claims are not countable against the driver, such as towing expenses or weather-related claims. But the rates will skyrocket if you have more than three claims associated with a theft, collision, or bodily injury. Violations, no matter how small they are, always count against you. Depending on the insurance company, claims and driving record history can affect your insurance rates up to six years.

6. **Number of drivers and vehicles** on the policy. Insurance companies like policies that cover more than one vehicle and more than one driver. Multivehicle and multidriver discounts are very common. All drivers residing in the same household and all vehicles should be listed on the same policy. If a couple gets married, they should have only one personal auto policy for both drivers and all vehicles they own to save money with a multicar, multidriver discount. Assigning older vehicles to younger drivers will make premium rates better as well. How far and how often the vehicles are driven also make a difference. Most insur-

ance companies give a discount to vehicles labeled "pleasure" that are drivable less than four miles a day.

7. **The type of vehicle.** The insurance company codes every vehicle, which affects the rate. Expensive vehicles have higher rates than more affordable vehicles. Luxury vehicles will cost more to replace or repair, so the policy is rated accordingly. Vehicles with great safety features and that promise to protect the driver during the accident and thus reduce the number of bodily injury claims are also rated more favorably.

8. **Protection.** Does your vehicle have OnStar service? Does your vehicle have an alarm system or any other device that would protect your vehicle from being stolen? Insurance companies like when the owner of the vehicle is responsible enough to protect his property from being damaged, vandalized, or stolen. Where you keep your vehicle is also important. Garaged vehicles have better rates than those parked on the street, in school parking lots, or any other busy place where the vehicle is more exposed to damage.

Chapter 26

Fifteen Ways to Save On an Auto Insurance Premium

There are many ways to save on auto insurance. Here are some of them.

1. Place your auto, homeowner's, renters, and any other policy with the same company. The insurance company will give you a discount called a **companion discount**, and it can be from 10 percent to 20 percent, depending on the company. Always make calculations. Sometimes you can save more by having your auto and home insurance with different carriers. Auto policies usually are six-month policies, although there are some companies writing business for twelve months. Homeowner's policies are twelve-month policies. When you are calculating your expense, compare them by the monthly cost, not the annual premium.

2. Having more than one car insured with the same auto policy gives you a multicar discount.

3. Being married also gives you a discount. Insurance companies think that marriage makes people behave more responsibly.

4. Compare prices regularly with the same company or other companies. The insurance industry changes all the time, and you never know what is out there that's better for you. If you keep your policies with an independent agent who writes business with many companies, give him or her a call. The agent should shop for you.

5. Shop for your auto insurance early. Many companies give a nice discount on advance quoting. Asking for a quote eight to ten days before you want your policy to be effective makes a big difference.

6. Good student discounts give you an additional discount if your children are on the policy and they are good students. The insurance company will need a copy of the grades. So when you tell your agent to give you that discount, make sure you know that your kids have good grades.

7. Most companies run your credit score, driving record, and previous insurance history (claims) at the time the quote is made. Some insurance companies don't do that to save money. So when you are asking for a quote, tell the agent the truth so you will get a precise quote. Reports still will be run at the time when the policy is issued and will affect the rate.

8. Keep your credit score clean. Depending on the state and the insurance company, your credit score can help you or harm you. A high credit score number helps you get a significantly lower premium. If your credit score is not that good, don't tell the agent your social security number; some quotes can be run without it.

9. Pay your premium in advance. Paying semiannually or annually in full saves you money on auto insurance. Companies give good discounts for policies that are paid in full. You lose money when you choose to pay your premium monthly. Insurance companies charge you additional $2 to $5 per month just for processing fees. Moreover, always pay your bills on time. Insurance companies charge late fees.

10. Keep continuous insurance. Insurance companies don't like a lapse of more than thirty days. If you still have a loan, your auto policy should be kept in good standing for the life of the loan. If the policy is cancelled, the mortgagee will force their insurance on you, and that is much more expensive.

11. Increase the deductibles. The higher the deductibles, the lower the premium. Just make sure that you have money in savings to cover a claim that is lower than your deductible.

12. Pay smaller claims yourself; submit only bigger claims to the company. It doesn't matter how small or big your claim is, it is still on your record and will increase your premium on renewal.

13. If you are female more than twenty-one years old or a male at least twenty-five years old, or if you have children on your policy that just turned these ages, ask your agent to rerun the quotes for you again. Insurance companies have higher rates for males less than twenty-five years old and for females less than twenty-one years old.

14. Having theft preventative devices on the car or an alarm system in the house not only helps to keep the thieves away but also gives you a discount on your insurance. If you have alarm, active disabling device, or passive disabling device on your car, tell the agent and ask for a discount.

15. Take group discounts. If you are a member of AAA, AARP, ABA, AMA, or others, let the agent doing the quote know. If you or your parents are in the military, try getting insurance from USAA. They are good with premiums and specifically accommodate military personnel.

Chapter 27
Personal Auto Insurance Basics

A personal auto policy covers an individual involved in an accident. It is very important to be correctly insured against accidents that cause property damage or personal injury, no matter whom or what caused the damage.

State Laws and Auto Insurance

Each state requires drivers to carry adequate insurance limits in case of an accident to cover the losses. Insurance should be purchased from an agent authorized to sell insurance for the particular state where the vehicle is registered. For example, if the vehicle is registered in state of Oregon, it can't be insured by a Kansas insurance policy. Let's say you have two cars. One is garaged in Oregon, and the other is in Kansas. Although you own both cars, they should be registered in two different states and carry different insurance policies.

It is common for states to have different minimum coverage limits calculated to be sufficient limits to cover financial responsibility. What if you travel to visit your family with your car to another state? The out-of-state provision modifies the coverage to fit the particular state the insured is traveling through. Let's say the state that you live in has a coverage minimum of 30/60/30, but the state that you are visiting has a minimum limit of 50/100/50. Unfortunately, you get in an accident. The insurance company will count your policy limit being as 50/100/50, and you will be covered up to that amount.

Since each state has its own laws governing personal auto insurance requirements, please check the specifics of your policy with your current insurance agent.

People Insured on the Policy

The **named insured** listed on the declaration page is the person who makes decisions on the policy. A spouse or a civil partner is also considered named insured. Other family members should be added to the policy as additional drivers. A family member is a person who is related to the insured and is also a resident of the insured's household. That includes anyone related by marriage, domestic partnership, blood, adoption, foster child, or ward. A domestic partner is a person at least eighteen years old, who made a declaration of a domestic partnership, is living with the insured, shares the responsibilities of the household, and has joint financial obligations. That does not include more than one person and cannot be a roommate of the insured.

One spouse should live with the other spouse in the same household to be insured under the same policy. If a separation occurs before policy expires, the spouse who lives away is still insured under the same policy for ninety days after the separation occurred. If the separation occurs in the middle of the policy, cancellation of the policy should be a mutual agreement between the couple. A cancellation request signed by both spouses should suffice to cancel the policy. After the policy expires or is canceled, both spouses can get their separate policies.

An auto policy also covers other persons who are not members of the household. These are called **other named insured**. Other named insured also can be another person who is not on the policy but is driving the insured's car with insured's permission. Let's say you were celebrating your anniversary at the restaurant, had couple of drinks, and your friend drives you home. He is covered under your policy.

Vicarious liability covers any person or organization responsible for any acts of the named insured and sharing the liability. It also covers any person or organization legally responsible for the omissions of a named insured. Here is an example. Let's say Richard is in a hurry after his lunch and is rushing to the meeting because he is already late. He doesn't notice Bob, who is turning around the corner into the parking lot, and hits his car. Since Richard was on a lunch break and rushing back to work, Bob sues Richard and his company for all the damages. Under these circumstances, Bob's personal auto policy also covers his company liability. If Richard were driving a company car when that happened, his personal auto policy would not cover his company liability. The employer needs to provide company auto insurance to the employees who are driving company's vehicles.

If you are selling a car, complete the title transfer yourself to make sure is done properly. Later on, if the car you sold is stolen or is involved in a crime, your name won't be on the title, and the police won't come for you.

Lienholders and Auto Insurance

If you are leasing a vehicle or making payments on a car, the leasing company or auto loan finance company will be listed on your policy as an additional insured or lienholder. Until the vehicle is paid for, the lienholder is also the owner of the vehicle and wants to make sure that their property is insured properly. Some finance companies require particular liability limits and deductibles to be listed on the policy. Please check with your finance company to make sure you have adequate coverage.

When you change insurance companies, please give the insurance company your lienholder information and your loan or reference number. Usually, the insurance company notifies your lienholder about the changes, but, just in case, contact your lienholder with the updated insurance information. If the lienholder does not have current insurance coverage information, the lienholder usually send a letter to you or the insurance company requesting information. If you received a letter from your lienholder and are not sure what to do, call your agent for help. A good agent will take care of it for you.

What Is Covered

Auto insurance covers the vehicles listed in the **declarations** portion of the policy. The insured must own the vehicles or must lease them under a long-term contract for six months or more. Vehicles eligible for the coverage include private passenger autos, which are four-wheel motor vehicles, and pickup trucks and vans under a certain weight that are not used for business. Since farming is not considered a business, any farm wagon or implements towed by the vehicle listed in the declarations are covered. Any trailers owned by the named insured and listed on the policy are also covered. A trailer is a vehicle designed to be pulled by a pickup, van, or a private passenger auto. Liability coverage carries over to the trailer from the insured car towing it. If the insured requests it, property damage coverage, such as collision and comprehensive, can be added to the policy by endorsement.

Any auto or trailer not owned by the named insured is also covered under the policy if it is used as temporary substitute for a vehicle shown in the declarations. For the substitute vehicle to be covered, the vehicle listed in the declarations should be out of use because of destruction, loss, servicing, repairs, or breakdown. Out of use does not mean the lack of availability because somebody else is using the car. For example, if Bob is out on a hunting trip, and Marsha, his wife, decides to go shopping and rents a car for that purpose, the insurance company will not reimburse rental expenses.

Occupying the vehicle means to be in a vehicle, around the vehicle, or getting into, onto, out of, or off the vehicle.

Teenagers and Auto Insurance

Adding a teenage driver to the family auto policy is expensive and painful. Rates double easily even with a clear driving record. Rates go down when the teenage boy reaches twenty-five and when a girl reaches twenty-one. After your child's birthday, call your agent and ask them to rerun the auto quotes for you. Rates can change to your favor.

If you have more drivers in the house than vehicles, you can add your teenager as an occasional driver instead of a principal driver. Giving an older car to your teenager to drive will also save you money on the insurance premium and on future repairs.

When your child gets a learner's permit, you don't have to add him or her to your policy because the student can't be driving on the street without a teacher. As soon the driver's license is received, the child should be added on the policy as an additional driver.

Even if your child is off to college, leave him or her on the policy. When holidays come or when it's summer, your teenager will be covered, even if a car is borrowed from a friend.

There are discounts for the policy:

► If the college student is a hundred miles or more away from home.

► If your child is a good student, averaging Bs, providing a report card will give you a discount.

► Depending on the insurance company, defensive driving certificates also can help you to reduce the premium, but to be sure, check that with your agent.

Replacing a Vehicle on the Policy

When you purchase a new car that replaces one listed in the declarations, the new auto automatically has the broadest coverage provided for any vehicle already listed in the declarations. If the new vehicle does not replace one that is already insured, you must request coverage within fourteen days after buying the new vehicle. For physical damage coverage, it doesn't matter if the new auto is a replacement or an additional auto. If you already have at least one car that is insured for physical damage, coverage begins on the date you get the auto, as long as you request to add it to your policy within fourteen days of acquiring it. The new auto will then automatically have the broadest coverage provided for any vehicle already listed in the declarations.

If you do not have physical damage on your policy already, the coverage for the new auto needs to be requested within four days of the getting the new auto. If a loss occurs in the time before the insured requests the coverage, a $500 deductible applies. If you are asking to add that coverage on the policy and a new auto after the four or fourteen days pass, then the new auto coverage is added effective the day you request it to be effective.

For example, Monica has a 2005 Toyota. Her liability limits are $50,000/$100,000, and the property damage limit is $50,000. Collision has a $500 deductible; anything other than collision is also $500. Monica replaces this car with new one, a 2011 Ford. Her liability coverage for the newly acquired vehicle is covered automatically, but to active collision and other than collision coverage, she needs to request the coverage from the insurance agent within fourteen days of buying the 2011 Ford. Let's say Monica does not have collision coverage, comprehensive or no coverage at all. The new car should be insured for that coverage within four days of buying it.

Company Vehicle

If you drive a company auto to work, your employer should provide you with the insurance for that car. A commercial auto policy your company purchases covers you in case of liability for injuries and property damage you cause to others, or even if you rent, borrow, or drive another company car only for company business. This type of policy has exclusions and does not cover any losses if you borrow, rent, or use the car for personal purposes. If you injure a coworker riding with you in the company car, the company insurance won't cover that either.

That is why it is important to have a personal auto policy covering any other cars you drive and other drivers in your household. If you want to protect yourself from liability, such as from injuring a coworker in the example, you can add a nonowner auto endorsement to your personal policy. In addition, an umbrella policy can cover injuries you cause to coworkers while using the company car. Please read more about umbrella coverage in Chapter 37, or call your agent to learn more about an umbrella quote. You also can have your employer add a broad form, Drive Other Cars endorsement to a business auto policy, which covers your liability while driving borrowed or rented vehicles.

If you don't own a separate vehicle for your personal use outside your company time, you should purchase a nonowner personal auto policy to cover you while you are driving company's vehicle outside your work hours.

Nonowner Insurance

A nonowner personal auto policy covers a person who does not own any vehicle at all, but occasionally uses somebody else's vehicle to commute or run errands. For example, Bridget doesn't own a car; she takes the bus to work every day. Occasionally, when she needs it, she borrows her neighbor's car to run some errands. Bridget also has a sister who lets her drive a car once in awhile. Obviously, Bridget can't be additional driver on all her friends' and siblings' auto policies. And just in case not every vehicle Bridget drives is properly insured, she should purchase a nonowner insurance policy.

Bailee and Your Vehicle

A bailee is someone who has been entrusted with another person's property, usually to repair or service it. "No benefit to bailee" means the insurance company will not pay to repair any of the damages to the property in a bailee's possession. For example, you took your car to the shop to be repaired. A couple days later, when you are picking up your car, you notice that there is a big scratch on the door. Don't submit a claim to your insurance company; it won't be covered. The repair shop is responsible for the scratch, and their commercial insurance policy should cover to repair the damage.

Cancelling the Auto Policy

A **termination** provision describes the conditions for cancellation and nonrenewal of the policy. You can cancel auto policy at any time by submitting a written letter to the insurance company with the effective day you want to cancel. There is no need to wait until the policy reaches the renewal date.

Some people think, "Well, I just won't pay for the renewal, and policy will cancel automatically." Don't wait for your policy to be canceled for nonpayment. That will harm your relationship with the insurance company and leave a bad record. In the future, if you come back to the same company, the company already has a record of you as an insured that doesn't pay, and your rates will be higher.

Check your payment plan before canceling the policy. Most policies today are set up with an automatic payment plan, so the renewal premium can be already taken from your account, and you will be still waiting on that policy cancellation. Cancel the policy as far ahead of time as possible. Some insurance companies submit a payment request to your bank at least ten days before the actual due date. Of course, the insurance company will return that premium by depositing it back to your account or by sending you a refund check. But that will take time. Check with your agent as to how the cancellation and refund will be handled in your case.

The insurance company cannot cancel or not renew your policy without written notice. The insurance company has to notify you in writing at least ten days before the effective day of the cancellation for nonpayment or if the cancellation occurs within the first sixty days of a newly issued policy.

After the policy has been issued and in effect for sixty days, the insurance company can cancel the policy only if the insured is not paying for the policy, has made a fraudulent claim, or misrepresented something when obtaining the policy. A policy can be canceled if the operator of the vehicle has had his driver's license or car registration suspended or revoked. Any household resident or person who drives any auto on the policy is subject to the same provision. Such a driver should be excluded from the policy, or the insurance company has a right to cancel the policy. Nonrenewal requires at least twenty days advance notice; some companies go as far as ninety days before the nonrenewal will go into effect. Please check this with your agent.

Exclusions

The following items are not covered under the insurance policy.

▶ Wear and tear losses

▶ Regular maintenance expenses, such as oil changes, inspection, freezing, mechanical, or electrical breakdown.

▶ Failure to maintain, such as if you damaged the engine because you forgot to change the oil in your car.

▶ Tire wear.

▶ Cosmetic changes to the car. Don't call your agent to submit a claim because you want to paint your rims.

▶ If you installed a DVD player for your kids in the car and did not tell your agent about it, it is not covered.

▶ Tapes, CDs, DVDs, and other media also not covered.

▶ Damages from war or nuclear perils, and damaged caused by government or civil authorities.

▶ Autos being used for public convenience, delivery, carpooling business use, taxi, limo, delivery, courier, or a prearranged racing or speed contest.

▶ Electronic equipment that reproduces, receives, or transmits audio and video, radar, or laser-detection equipment or data signals are not covered, unless the equipment came from the factory and is installed permanently. Special equipment needs to be insured with a special equipment endorsement. There is no way an agent will know what you purchased and added to your vehicle if you don't tell him. If you bought those fancy rims and the car is stolen, and those rims did not come from the Cadillac factory, and you added no endorsement, it is not covered.

Campers, motor homes, and trailers have their own exclusions.

▶ If the damage occurred to a camper body, motor home, or trailer that is not listed in the declarations, it is not covered.

▶ Damages to cooking, dining, plumbing, or refrigeration facilities.

▶ Awnings, cabanas, or equipment designed to create additional living space.

Losses are also excluded to a nonowned auto when used by the named insured or family members without a reasonable belief that he or she is entitled to do so. This means if somebody steals the car from your house, your insurance won't cover the person who stole the car.

Chapter 28

What an Auto Policy Covers

Many insurance companies provide personal auto coverage. There are similarities and differences, so it is important to become familiar with the coverage a particular insurance company is offering before you buy an insurance policy from them. Of course, there are elements common to all policies. An auto policy covers travel in the United States, its territories, and its possessions, including Canada and Puerto Rico. Some policies cover up to twenty miles into Mexico. Vehicles being transported between those territories are also covered.

If the law regulating insurance coverage changes, the policy automatically changes too. Usually, an insurance company makes the change without asking the insured and without an additional charge. Please check your personal auto policy so you know how your insurance company handles coverage.

All insurance companies issue personal auto policies that include four standard parts:

- ► Part A, liability coverage
- ► Part B, medical payments or personal injury protection coverage

► Part C, uninsured/underinsured motorists coverage

► Part D, physical damage to your auto

All four parts and an additional endorsement such as towing or roadside assistance, make a full coverage policy. Parts of the policy can be added or removed per an insured's request. Some parts of the policy cannot exist without the other parts. For example, Part B, medical payments coverage, cannot exist without Part A, liability. Part C, uninsured motorist's coverage, may be included in the policy together with Part A, liability coverage, depending on state law. The coverage limit for the policy is shown on the declarations page and the premium charged. The four parts are discussed below.

Part A, Liability Coverage

Liability coverage defends the insured and covers bodily injury and property damage losses that the insured is legally liable for. This coverage promises to defend the insured in a suit and to pay any defense costs as far as the policy limits will allow. Liability coverage is the cornerstone of every policy. Having only Part A on your policy makes the auto policy valid for liability only and would not include any of the other parts.

The **Bodily Injury Liability (BI)** section of Part A covers damages for another person's injuries, sickness, disease, or death caused by vehicles or drivers listed on the policy. It also covers someone who is driving the insured vehicle with the insured's permission. This coverage pays for medical bills, lost wages, and the pain and suffering of the other person injured by the insured. It also covers legal fees, bail bonds, or court costs that might incur in the process to settle the claim. It is critical to have sufficient liability limits to cover such losses. If you don't, you will pay these costs out of your pocket. Your future earnings also can be claimed to pay for the losses.

The **Property Damage Liability (PD)** coverage pays for the other person's damaged property that was damaged by the at-fault accident of the insured, the other driver, or vehicle listed on the policy. Damage can be anything, including vehicle, signs, buildings, bushes, or any personal property. It's very important to carry more than the state minimum limits on your policy. If the accident involves more than one car, your personal assets and earnings, including your salary and savings, can be at risk to pay for the losses. An umbrella policy will give you an additional liability coverage; that is discussed in Chapter 37.

The **Limits of Liability** listed in the policy can be provided on a Combined Single Limit basis. It combines bodily injury and property damage into one limit. The most common limits of liability are displayed on a split limit basis. The limits are usually expressed as a series of three numbers, such as 50/100/25. This means, in case of an accident, the policy will pay $50,000 per person for the bodily injury, $100,000 per accident bodily injury no matter how many persons are injured, and $25,000 per accident for property damage caused to the other vehicle. Let's say Dylan's personal auto policy liability limits are 100/300/100, and after an accident, there is a $150,000 judgment against Dylan for the injuries caused to one person. In this case, the policy will pay $100,000 up to the limits of the policy. Dylan needs to come up with the rest of the $50,000 himself. If four people were injured at the time of the accident, then the liability limit of $300,000 would be divided between the four, making it $75,000 for each person.

Exclusions

If an insured damages someone else's property and intentionally causes bodily injury, the insurance company will not provide coverage. The policy covers accidents, not intentional actions. So if Peter backs into his mother's car, which was parked in the driveway, and both vehicles are listed on the policy, insurance won't cover that.

Coverage is also declined if the property is rented or is in use by someone in care of insured. Let's say you rent a small tractor from the home improvement store to dig in your backyard. Or perhaps you rent a trailer. These incidents are not covered under your auto policy.

The policy also excludes any losses caused by the insured using the vehicle as a public conveyance, such as taxi, limo service, or courier. If you are using your vehicle and getting money for the service, you should have commercial auto policy. Carpooling with a couple of coworkers is not considered public conveyance, and the policy covers it. Motorized vehicles with less than four wheels or that are designed to be used off public roads are not covered under the personal auto policy.

The vehicle listed on the policy will not be covered if it is used without the insured's permission. For example, if the truck is stolen, the policy will not cover any of the thief's damage.

Bodily injury and property damage will not be covered if can be covered under another liability policy. Vehicles not added to the policy after fourteen days of purchase by any insured's family member listed on the policy are not covered. So make sure you notify your agent of the new vehicle and insure the properly correctly. When the policy is changed, your premium payment can increase or decrease, depending on the new vehicle, coverage, and other factors.

Part B, Medical Payments or Personal Injury Protection Coverage

Liability coverage in Part A covers a person in the other vehicle. Part B covers you. This coverage provides protection for anyone in the vehicle, entering the vehicle, or struck by the vehicle during the time of the accident. It can be the insured, family members, or other passengers not related to the insured. It covers people present at the time of the accident in the insured's vehicle. No matter who is at fault, this coverage provides reasonable expenses for medical bills and even funeral services up to three years after the accident. For example, an oncoming vehicle struck Rosa's vehicle, and she is injured, as are her aunt and her aunt's friend. All three will be covered under the other driver's liability coverage, and in addition to that, all three are covered under Rosa's Part B medical payment coverage. If the accident is Rosa's fault, persons injured in the other car will be covered under Part A of her insurance policy.

Personal Injury Protection (PIP) is another coverage choice that extends medical payments coverage. An insured can't have this coverage and Part B on the policy; it can only be one or the other. This protection covers the insured, and his or her insurance policy pays for the loss. It does not cover the passengers in the other car that the insured struck. PIP coverage is available for anyone who is inside the car (with the insured's permission) or outside the car at the time of the accident, and anyone who is passing by, such a bicyclist. It doesn't matter whose fault the accident is.

Personal injury protection covers more than just medical payments. It includes X-rays, prosthetic devices, dental services, and hospital, nursing, and funeral expenses. It will extend the coverage to lost wages, up to 80 percent of actual income. PIP also covers maintenance of the household, such essential services like meals at a restaurant, a maid to clean a house, and an insured babysitter was injured and could not perform his or her duties. One person cannot collect the loss of essential services and lost income. This coverage is automatically included in the policy if the insured does not reject it. To find out more about this coverage, please contact your agent.

Limits of Liability

Part B coverage is a single limit liability applied in case of injuries each person sustained in one vehicle during one accident. Coverages are typically $1,000, $2,000, $2,500, $5,000, and $10,000. This coverage can be used only once and can't be covered by any other coverage, such as an underinsured motorist coverage. For example, three women are injured in an accident, and the insured's medical payment limit is $2,000. Sabrina's payments are $1,900, Barbara's are $2,000, and Kelley's expenses are $3,200. Sabrina's and Barbara's losses are paid in full, and Kelley only gets $2,000, because that is the limit on the coverage.

Exclusions for Part B are the same as those for Part A. Medical payments are not paid for losses caused by occupying a motor vehicle that has fewer than four wheels or for vehicles used for business or public convenience, such as a taxi. Such vehicles should be covered under a separate policy. Not covered vehicles also include vehicles that are not listed on the policy, even if the insured or family member of the insured owns vehicle. No vehicle is covered if someone is occupying the vehicle without insured permission or a reasonable belief that he or she is entitled to occupy it. Vehicles used for racing or speed contests are not covered. Any losses caused by war or nuclear hazard are also not covered. There is no coverage for intentional acts or for trying to evade the police.

Part C: Uninsured/Underinsured Motorist Coverage

Part C, Uninsured/Underinsured Motorist Coverage, pays for losses caused by a legally liable uninsured motorist (UM) or underinsured motorist (UIM). The loss must occur in an auto accident and must involve bodily injury or death to the insured, household relatives, or passengers. Punitive damages are excluded; only bodily injury is included. Some states add property damage to this coverage, so please check with your insurance provider. Part C losses can be paid when the accident with bodily injury and property damage happens to the insured from a vehicle that qualifies as an uninsured vehicle. For example, Teresa was walking across the street, and an unidentified car struck her and left the scene. That would be considered hit-and-run and falls under uninsured motorist coverage, because the driver could not be identified.

An **Uninsured Motor Vehicle** is a vehicle that does not have liability coverage at the time of the accident. For example, Jerry struck Clint. Jerry forgot to pay for his auto policy, which was canceled for nonpayment. At the time the accident occurred, Jerry had no insurance. If Clint has UM coverage, his losses are covered.

An **Underinsured Motor Vehicle** is the vehicle that has liability coverage but not enough to cover the losses. State minimum liability coverage usually is not enough to cover the losses. For example, Terry runs a stoplight and hits Ben's 2012 Mercedes Benz. Terry's liability limits are 30/60/30, and $30,000 won't be enough to cover the damages to Ben's vehicle. If Ben has UIM coverage, Terry's policy will pay up to $30,000, and Ben's policy will cover the rest.

Uninsured/Underinsured Motorist Bodily Injury provides two limits of coverage. The first number, 50/100/50, is the maximum amount that the insurance company will pay for the injury or death to any one person. In the given example, this is $50,000. The second number, $100,000, is the maximum that the insurance company will pay for injury or death in a single occurrence. No matter how many people are injured, all of them will share that $100,000. The more people injured in the accident, the less the amount to cover them. That is why it is very important to carry as high of a limit as you can.

Any person, such as an insured on the policy, the family member, or anyone occupying the vehicle at the time of the accident, is covered under Uninsured/Underinsured Motorist's coverage. The person doesn't even have to be in the vehicle. It can be, let's say, the spouse of the someone who received bodily injury. The spouse can make a claim for loss of companionship and loss of services, such as babysitting and housekeeping duties, and even loss of sex.

Uninsured/Underinsured Motorist Property Damage pays for the damages the insured is legally entitled to recover when the uninsured and underinsured motorist causes the damage. This coverage is mandatory in some states, so please check with your agent. If it is not mandatory, it can be chosen as one of the coverages on the policy or added as an endorsement after the policy is already issued. Every state applies different minimum limits in case of a loss. Usually, this coverage does not cover the first $250 of damage to the insured's vehicle.

There are agents out there who say you don't need underinsured motorist coverage because you already have comprehensive and collision coverage on your policy. Everyone should be carrying enough insurance, but plenty of drivers only have state minimum liability limits and can't cover the losses that they cause. What if there is more than one car involved? The state minimum limits will not be enough to cover all the losses, and you are stuck repairing your own car. You can submit a claim under your collision coverage, but that will increase your rates on renewal. Adding this coverage will not increase your premium that much, but it will make a huge difference when you get in an accident with the underinsured motorist. For example, David's auto policy carries underinsured motorist coverage up to $100,000. David gets in an accident, and it is Marabel's fault. Unfortunately, Marabel has only $50,000 liability coverage, and David suffers bodily injury of $75,000. So Marabel's policy will cover up to $50,000, and David's underinsured policy coverage will pay the rest of $25,000.

Exclusions are the same as other exclusions mentioned in Parts A and B.

Part D, Physical Damage Coverage

Part D covers the insured's car. This coverage provides Collision and Other than Collision, also called Comprehensive, coverages. **Collision** covers the vehicle involved in the collision with another object, whether it is another vehicle, a curb, or a tree. It also includes upset, which is when a car leaves the road, rolls down an embankment, and lands on its top. This coverage comes with deductible that can be as low as $250 and high as $1,500, depending on the insurance company. Excluded from this coverage are falling objects, theft or larceny, vandalism, civil commotion, hail, windstorm, flood, fire, explosion, earth movement, breakage of glass, or contact with a bird or animal. Those losses are covered under other sections, not collision coverage.

Other Than Collision Losses or Comprehensive coverage covers all other damages not covered under collision coverage, such as fire, windstorm, hail, water, flood, breakage of glass, contact with a bird or animal, missiles or falling objects, theft or larceny, malicious mischief or vandalism, riot or civil commotion, and explosion or earthquake. To cover glass breakage caused by the collision, the insured can treat it as a collision loss to avoid double deductible, rather than filing it under Comprehensive coverage. For example, if an auto slides on an icy bridge, runs into a curb, and flips onto its side, or if the auto stops on the freeway, causing the other cars behind to crash into it as a chain reaction, then it is a Collision claim. Let's say a cow escapes from a farm and wanders onto the highway, and the auto runs into the cow. It is an Other Than Collision or Comprehensive claim. Other examples: the auto is stolen from a parking lot, a bird flies into the windshield, or the auto is swept away in a flood.

Exclusions

There are circumstances when auto policy coverage is excluded.
- Wear and tear.
- Freezing of the auto.

- Mechanical breakdown.
- Road damage to tires.
- Nuclear mishaps.
- Contaminated groundwater.
- Vehicles used as livery conveyance, such as taxi or limo.
- Vehicles used for delivery of newspapers, magazines, food, or courier.
- Farm machinery.
- Vehicles with fewer than four wheels.
- Vehicles with other auto insurance.
- Businesses that repair, sell, service, or store the vehicle should get garage coverage form.
- Vehicle can't be used as a residence.
- Vehicles the government confiscated.
- Property in control or custody of the insured is not covered.
- Any equipment not permanently installed in the vehicle, if not added by endorsement.
- Loss of electronic sound reproducing equipment, such as radios and CD and DVD players.
- Loss of any video, audio data, telephones, scanning monitors, TV monitors, personal computers, any tapes, and records that accompany such equipment is not covered. It is covered under a homeowner's or renter's policy that covers personal property.

Endorsements

Any change on the policy can be done by endorsement. Endorsements should indicate when the change should be effective. If the insurance company makes the policy form broader, the policyholder will receive better coverage without an additional premium automatically the effective day of that change.

Some insureds need special coverages added to their policy.

- A **joint ownership** coverage endorsement states that the policy can be issued to two or more people who live in the same household or two or more people who are related in another way besides being spouses. For example, Monica moved to college, but her and her mother own the vehicle. Monica can add her mother's name as joint owner on the policy, since both of them own the vehicle.

▶ **Towing and labor** endorsement reimburses the insured for the cost of having vehicle towed and the labor performed at the place of disablement. The labor done after towing into garage or auto shop is not covered. The basic coverage limit is $25, but it can be as high as $50 per day. Sometimes, it is better to go with big companies that specialize in roadside assistance, such as AAA. You should compare the coverage and the price to make a decision about including such service in your policy.

▶ Many insurance companies provide **roadside assistance**. This coverage is very affordable, around $25 per year, depending on the company. It includes towing to the closest repair shop, change of a tire at the breakdown place, key lock-out service, jumping a battery, and delivery of water, fuel, oil or other needed fluids, although the cost of those fluids is not included. Just as with towing and labor coverage, you might choose to use AAA or other provider and decline the insurance company coverage.

▶ **Miscellaneous vehicle** endorsements include adding coverage for special recreational vehicles such as golf carts, motor homes, motorcycles, all-terrain vehicles, dune buggies, golf carts, and mopeds. Some companies have specialized policies to cover these vehicles.

▶ **An optional limits transportation expenses** coverage endorsement allows the insured to choose the daily and maximum limits of coverage provided for transportation or loss of use expenses for scheduled or nonowned vehicles, such as renting a car when covered auto is out of service. This endorsement pays a minimum of $20 and maximum $600.

▶ An **excess electronic equipment** endorsement adds coverage for things like records, tapes, CDs, and DVDs and increases the limit of insurance for electronic equipment permanently installed in an area of the auto not normally used for installing this equipment.

▶ The **named nonowner** coverage endorsement may be issued to someone who doesn't own an automobile but who drives borrowed or rented autos. It can be used for the insured who drives a corporate car the company provides for him. While the insured is driving a company car, he is covered under the company car insurance, but as soon he drives a car other than the company car, he is not covered. This endorsement will cover the gap. For example, Martin's employer provided him with a company car that he uses to commute to work and to meet the clients. After work hours, when Martin is not working, the company's insurance policy has no effect, but he uses company car to run his personal errands. This endorsement will cover him after work hours.

Customized Vehicles and Antiques

Customized cars are popular now, with additional TVs, DVD players, custom paint jobs, carpeting, high-end stereos, slide-in campers, pickup toppers for wheelchairs, and even refrigerators. If it did not come from the manufacturer, it is not covered under a personal auto policy. At the time of the quote, make sure you mention that to the agent and give the amount how much such things would cost. Keep the receipts for the future, just in case a claim appears, such as fire, flood, vandalism or collision, or theft.

There are insurance companies that specialize only in insuring classic cars. You also can add a classic car to your personal auto policy with other cars. Usually, an insurance company asks you to send pictures of the car to the insurance company with the appraisal. If you insure it for stated-amount coverage, the vehicle will be insured up to that amount. Let's say you insured it at $15,000, and if the vehicle is ever declared as a total loss, the insurance company will send you a check for $15,000, even though the actual cash value on that car is just $12,000.

If the auto is insured on an actual cash value basis, the insurance company will pay you the Kelley Blue Book value. The Kelley Blue Book is a nationwide auto valuation service and will state how much your car was worth at the time based on several factors. Let's say the market value of your car is $10,000. That is how much you will get, not the $15,000 you insured it for. Keep all the receipts, pictures, and appraisals for your records. If something happens, you can submit all the paperwork to the adjuster and be paid a higher amount than the Kelley Blue Book value.

You've probably heard of **gap insurance.** Dealerships ask you to purchase this policy. If you don't purchase it from the dealership, you also can do this with your insurance agent. Auto Loan/Lease Coverage will pay off what is left of the loan if the car is totaled. For example, let's say Veronica buys a car and the new vehicle cost her $20,000. As soon she drives off the parking lot, the vehicle loses value, and the Kelley Blue Book value is less than what the car was purchased for. Let's say she already paid $4,000 toward her loan and gets in the accident. Her car is totaled. The insurance company pays the claim based on the Kelley Blue Book value, which is $13,000. At the end, she has no car and is stuck with $3,000 that she still owes on the loan. If she has gap insurance coverage, the insurance company will pay off the loan in full, no matter what the Kelley Blue Book value is. Adding such coverage doesn't cost that much. Depending on the state and insurance company, it can be $20 to $50 a year. It's worth considering if you have a loan on your car.

Dropping Coverage

When people pay off a car, they commonly decide to drop the uninsured/underinsured coverage or comprehensive and collision coverage. If you have enough money in a savings account to buy a new car or have another vehicle on the policy that can be available for you right away, go ahead.

Supplementary Payments

These are paid in addition to the limits listed on the declarations page. Those payments include up to $250 or more for the cost of bail bonds due to an auto accident. A personal auto policy defends any bonds to release attachments in the suit, premiums on appeal bonds, and interest accruing after a judgment. Appeal bonds are required to make sure that the person will appear in court and will be able to pay the amount that the court will determine for the damages. Sometimes the court will lock up or attach the insured's property to make sure that the insured will put up a bond to guarantee the payment. Supplementary payments also include up to $200 a day for loss of earnings and traveling expenses due to hearings the insured attends at the insurance company's request.

Chapter 29

Auto Claims

G etting into an auto accident is an unfortunate event no matter whose fault it is. There are only two ways to get in an accident— through your fault or somebody else's fault. Most of the time, you did nothing wrong, you were the obeying driver, but through an unlucky twist of circumstances, you end up with damages to your property. Sometimes damages don't include the other driver. Submitting a claim and getting your losses paid can be a painful experience. This is the time when you assess how good your agent is and how well your property is insured. In the case of at-fault accident, the damages to your property are covered under the other person's policy. If the other person's insurance company can't cover the loss, your insurance policy should cover the rest, with no gaps that you end up paying for.

Submitting a Claim to Your Insurance Company

If you get in an accident and it is your fault, your car will be repaired or replaced by your collision coverage, if you have it. Before submitting any claim, you should first contact your agent and ask for advice on that.

If the agent advises you to go with the claim, there are two ways to submit a claim to your insurance company:

1. You can submit the claim through your agent

2. You can submit it directly to your company by calling a claims number. This is the preferable choice because there are things about the loss that only you know about, and your agent won't be able to answer the questions the claims department representative will ask.

If you submit a claim, remember that any loss is subject to a deductible, and any claim you submit to the insurance company needs to be higher than the amount of the deductible. If the repair can be done for less than your deductible or for a little bit higher, pay for the repairs out of your pocket. Paying for your small repairs will prevent increasing premiums on renewal. For example, Mitchell is about to submit a comprehensive claim. He hit a large branch while driving at night. His comprehensive deductible is $500. If the damage is less than $500, Mitchell will need to repair the damage himself. If the damage is higher than $500, Mitchell can consider submitting a claim. But Mitchell doesn't want to increase his premium next year, so he pays for the repairs himself, even if the damage is more than $500.

If you did not get into an accident and there is no other person at fault, and it was not a hit-and-run accident, be careful when submitting a claim to your insurance company. Remember, any maintenance claims are not covered under auto policy. Don't call your agent and ask to submit a claim to repaint your vehicle, buy new tires, or change oil. There are insurance agents that will submit a claim for you without recommending you the opposite. Any submitted claim, even when it is declined, is still considered a claim and can affect your future premium. A good agent can analyze your problem and give you an advice about submitting the claim.

Windshield cracks are a common cause for claims. If your vehicle windshield cracked, and the crack is less than the length of a dollar bill, any windshield repair place can take care of it. If the crack is longer than a dollar bill, the windshield needs to be replaced by your comprehensive coverage. Before you submit a claim, get a couple of quotes for how much will cost you to replace the windshield. This kind of loss is also subject to a deductible, so before submitting a claim, know your deductibles and evaluate if paying for the windshield replacement yourself will save money.

Stolen cars are another cause for claims. When a car is stolen, most of the time, the car is recovered later but with damage. Your insurance company will wait couple of weeks before totaling your car to make sure that the car will not be recovered. Even if the car is later found, the insurance company can charge you only the theft deductible, not collision. During this waiting time, you should use a rental car or other transportation covered under the loss of use coverage. Because there is a long wait until the insurance company will pay for the total loss, some companies actually give a small rental coverage, so check with your agent.

The insurance company must notify you in writing when a claim against you was filed and inform you about the initial offer to settle a claim no later than ten days after the offer was made. After the settlement is done, the insurance company has thirty days to notify you about the settlement of the claim.

Submitting a Claim to another Insurance Company

An insurance company decides to choose whether to repair your damaged car, replace it with a new one, or pay you cash. The insurance company always calculates how much it will cost to declare your vehicle a total loss or to repair your vehicle. Physical damage losses are calculated on the cash value basis. Cash value basis is calculated by taking the amount your car costs when new and applying depreciation cost over time. It is important to know that the loss is paid on whichever is less, to replace or repair.

For example, Nick has a vehicle that he loves, and the insurance company is totaling it. There is no way Nick will talk them into fixing it and spending $10,000, when the actual Kelley Blue Book value is $7,000. The insurance company will pay Nick $7,000, and there is not much he can do about it. Unless he can provide the adjuster with other appraisal values from other appraisal books and prove that the vehicle is worth more, Nick's settlement will be $7,000.

If the other person is at fault and causes damage to your car in the accident, you can collect the repair costs from the other person's liability coverage or from your own collision coverage. Your collision coverage pays for the damage to your car no matter whose fault it is. If you submit the claim to your insurance company, it is possible the claim will be solved faster than through the other person's insurance company. When you file a claim on your auto policy, your insurance provider will pay the deductible back to you after the repairs are done. In addition, you don't have to deal with subrogation or comparative negligence.

As mentioned earlier, **subrogation** is when your legal rights to seek reimbursement from the other driver are transferred to your insurance company. So you use your deductible. Your insurance company pays for your damage and goes after the other person's insurance to be reimbursed for the damage.

Comparative negligence is when the fault is assessed to more than one person. If you hit a parked car, it is 100 percent your fault. But if you rear-end a car on the street, then there is a chance that the driver in front of you also had something to do with causing the accident. Please check with your agent; every state has different rules.

Your Duties after Loss

The **Conditions** portion of your personal auto policy lists your duties after an accident. Please become familiar with them, so if the time comes to use them, you will know how to react. Duties after the accident or any damage to the vehicle are the same as with any other personal property.

- ▶ First, notify the police, especially if the vehicle is damaged in an accident or hit-and-run incident or is stolen.
- ▶ Write the personal information of the person whose fault it is and any witnesses still there. Collect their names, driver's license numbers, addresses, and phone numbers.
- ▶ Collect the other driver's insurance information, such as the insurance company name, phone number, and policy number.

- ► If you have a cell phone with the capability to take pictures, take photos. The more documentation you have to show to the adjuster, the better.
- ► Contact the insurance company with precise details about the accident indicating how, where, and when the loss happened. Your description of the accident, your complaints, and any answers to the adjuster's questions will be recorded. Depending on the insurance company, the person who will take your personal information won't ask you about the accident. They just register you for the next available adjuster, who will contact you later.
- ► At the end of the conversation with the insurance claims department, you will be given a claim number as well as possibly your adjuster's name and phone number. Write this information down and keep it for communication between you and the adjuster.

If possible, damaged property should be protected against additional damage. If there are expenses that the insured pays to keep property protected, the insurance company will reimburse the expense. Later on, an adjuster will contact you, inspect the damages, and write a check to cover the repairs.

Adjusters

Don't think that your agent will tell you how the claim will be handled or how big of a check you should expect. The agent deals with the selling part of the insurance, and adjusters or claim specialists have nothing to do with sales. There are even different licenses for sales and claims. Most adjusters are knowledgeable about coverage and how much things would cost. You might push for more explanation as to how they arrived to the amount they are giving for a total loss or repairs.

After you submit a claim, write the claim number, your adjuster's name, and the phone number down. If it is possible, also get the claims department supervisor's name and number. Depending on the insurance company, it is almost impossible to reach your adjuster, so don't be surprised if you are directed to his or her voicemail. If you adjuster disappears for a week, and you can't contact him, call your agent and ask for help. A good agent will always try to help you.

You also can ask the claims department representative how your claim is being handled. The notes on your file should be enough for the person on the other line to tell you how far in the process your claim is and what your adjuster's last activity was on your file.

Getting Paid For the Loss

It is good idea to get the estimate yourself for your used car, and then wait until the adjuster gives you a number. Just look for the similar used cars in the dealerships like yours, and get the opinion of at least three places. Ask for used car managers and bring the pictures of your car. Write down their names, addresses, and contact numbers where they can be reached. When the adjuster gives you the amount of money for your car, you can dispute it with the evidence. The numbers also to keep in mind are sales tax, title fees, and prorated license registration fee until the month your license should have expired. Or you can file the claim against your own insurance and the other person's insurance and wait to see which insurance company will come up with a better offer.

After the claim is submitted, the adjuster will do the inspection himself and write the estimate. Sometimes the adjuster will ask for an appraisal. Most of the time, insurance companies have a list of the shops that they recommend, and usually the shops are well run. Either way, the choice of the repair shop handling the repair of your vehicle is up to you. Just be sure that the shop making the estimate is reasonable and not trying to rip the insurance company off. Get a couple of estimates to make sure that the appraisals given to you are fair. Adjusters have their own appraisal calculators and can tell immediately when the appraisal is too high.

Because your car experienced wear and tear, the insurance company has a right to replace damaged parts with used parts in good condition because wear and tear is not covered in the policy. So there are only two ways to deal with that. First, agree to the used parts or second, pay out of your own pocket for the difference between used and new parts, especially if the car is new.

There are situations when the adjuster mails you a check for the repairs, but when you take the car to the shop, it turns out that this check will not cover the costs. An adjuster can miss things that can be uncovered only when it is inspected by the shop that will do the repair. Get an estimate for how much more money will be needed to do the repairs and ask the adjuster to mail you another check. Of course, the adjuster will require proof from the repair shop and an estimate for how much is needed to finish the repairs. Never accept the check without the shop promising to fix the car for that amount of money. The amount of the check from the insurance company and repair shop estimate should be the same amount.

Let's say an adjuster already approved the additional check for the repairs, but the check itself has not arrived yet. Obviously, you want to get your vehicle back, but the repair shop is not allowing you to do that before the full payment is received. There is a specific form authorizing the insurer to issue the check directly to the shop for the rest of the repair. That should take care of the problem. After this form is signed, the shop should allow you to take the car. If the shop still doesn't want to give your car back, and you just can't do without it, a credit card or savings can be handy to pay the rest of the repair. Of course, the balance you pay to the shop will be reimbursed by the insurance company.

Signing the authorization also takes care of any additional repairs that the shop can come up with, eliminating any possibility of ripping you off. Any reputable shop will know that any part and any repair needs to be authorized or the adjuster won't pay. By signing this authorization, you are out of the equation, and the shop will need to prove to the adjuster that the additional amount of money was really needed. At that point, the discrepancy about the amount is not your problem.

Total Loss

A **total-loss claim** is when your car costs more to repair than it is worth. Remember, that the value is an actual cash value determined by the Kelley Blue Book value as a guide. Total loss is calculated by determining how valuable you car is before the accident versus how much the car will cost to repair it. There is a secondary consideration for the insurance company: the amount of money that the salvage yard will pay to the insurance company to collect your car.

Therefore, if repairing the car would cost $4,000, and the actual car value is $5,000, it can look like the insurance company should repair your car. However, if the salvage yard will pay $1,200, then the insurance company is better off totaling your car and paying you the actual cash value. You can get the cash value for your totaled car and keep the car for later repairs, if the car is so dear to you. All you will need to do is to pay the insurance company what it would get from the salvage yard so the insurance company doesn't lose anything.

If you think that the amount given to you is not fair, go to the dealership and ask them to give you two prices for your car: a used car before and after the accident. If the difference between those two numbers is more than the insurance company gave you, you can submit a claim for additional payment. But that is only if you decide not to repair the car. You need to remember that the value is less than the repair costs.

For example, Claudia got into an accident, and her vehicle is totaled. The insurance company knows that to repair the car would cost them $8,000, but the Kelley Blue Book value is $6,500. Claudia wants to have the vehicle fixed and requests the insurance company pay for the repairs. If Claudia proves that there are other acceptable sources showing her vehicle is actually worth $8,000, then the insurance company should repair the vehicle.

If your claim is denied or underpaid by your insurance company, it would seem the claim is handled wrong. But most of the time, the claim is either not covered by your policy or your policy has inadequate coverage.

You may consider suing the insurance company because you think the claim was handled unfairly. Please, remember that the insured cannot take legal action toward the insurance company until all of the policy terms have been complied with.

Chapter 30
Motorcycle Insurance

A s with any motor vehicle, a motorcycle also needs to have insurance. Insurance companies think of motorcycles as more risky than cars, and insurance rates can be higher than driving a regular car.

Do you have a motorcycle that you drive every day, or it is a motorcycle that is twenty years old and just kept as a collectible? The insurance you need will depend on how much you drive and what kind of the motorcycle it is.

Insurance rates depend on driving history, experience level, location, and pretty much the same factors used to calculate auto insurance rates. To find out more about it, please read Chapter 25. In addition to those factors, the type of motorcycle you drive also matters. High-powered sports motorcycles cost more to insure, because the liability is higher. Where you drive also matters, because riding a motorcycle in the city or in a high crime area always costs more.

If your motorcycle has tire locks or other devices that make motorcycle more safe in your absence, the insurance company can give a discount for that.

By law, every motorcycle should carry at least liability insurance. This coverage will cover damages to other people and injuries that the insured causes to other people. Liability only does not cover comprehensive or collision losses that would also cover the insured motorcycle. This part of insurance will increase the premium. It is a good idea to have the same high liability limit for motorcycle insurance as for any other insurance you have, such as home or auto. Don't forget to include the same liability limits for the passengers riding with you. Some agents would recommend the minimum medical or personal injury protection, because it is covered under health insurance, but I would recommend having more than less.

In case of a total loss, the insurance company will write you a check equal to Kelley Blue Book value. I would recommend keeping any receipts for your additional equipment on the motorcycle in case of a future claim. Receipts will prove your motorcycle's value, same as it does for a car.

If you have special equipment on your motorcycle, don't forget to mention that to your agent when getting a quote. Anything that you add after you purchase the motorcycle after it leaves the manufacturer needs to be insured. Don't assume that it is automatically insured.

Some motorcycle owners argue about a year-round policy versus a seasonal policy. Depending on the limits, most of the time, purchasing a year-round policy can cost the same as seasonal coverage. When shopping for a best rate, decide what coverage you want, get as many quotes as you can from different insurance companies, and compare them.

Classic Motorcycles

If you have a motorcycle considered a classic, you will need classic motorcycle insurance. Usually insurance companies think classic means old. A motorcycle needs to be fifteen or twenty years old to be considered a classic. Every insurance company has its own standards to determine that, so check with your insurance provider.

If you have a classic motorcycle collection but don't ride your motorcycles, you will need just theft and damages insurance policy. If you are planning to ride your classic motorcycle, then adding liability coverage is necessary.

It is a good idea to purchase classic motorcycle policy from an insurance company that specializes only in classic motorcycles. Some insurance companies insure classic motorcycles the same way as any other motorcycles, using the motorcycle's current value. Motorcycles, same as autos, lose their value over time. When there is a total loss, the standard insurance company will pay you how much your motorcycle is worth now by the Kelley Blue Book value. The amount can be very small compared to how much you paid for that motorcycle, leaving you unsatisfied. Classic motorcycle insurance companies cover a motorcycle for the agreed amount.

Chapter 31
Rental Vehicles

Y ou are liable for any injuries and property damage that you cause to another, regardless if you are driving your vehicle, a borrowed vehicle, or a rented vehicle. If you carry high coverage limits, your personal auto policy covers any losses no matter why you are driving a rental vehicle. There is confusion about what rental reimbursement covers and when this coverage is used.

When Rental Expenses Are Covered By Your Policy

Rental reimbursement covers a vehicle rented for the insured to use when the main vehicle listed on the policy is impossible to use because it is being repaired or serviced or is destroyed in an accident. For example, after your accident, your vehicle is the repair shop. You need to go to work, so you rent a vehicle to commute. Rental expenses will be reimbursed to you by your insurance company, if you have that kind of coverage.

This coverage does not cover the rental vehicles that you will use during a vacation or other purposes. It only kicks in if your vehicle received damages due the listed perils. Some households have more vehicles than drivers. In this case, if one auto is in the shop, they can use the other auto and don't choose to have this kind of coverage at all.

Rental reimbursement pays depending on the coverage that the insured chose at the time when policy was issued. Rental coverage reimbursement can go high as $50 per day and for long as for a month. This coverage would add about $30 per year for one vehicle.

If the insured can't use his or her vehicle because of the theft of the auto, there is a forty-eight hour waiting period before that coverage can be used. The rental car will be paid for by the insurance company until the vehicle is recovered or until the insurance company decides to repair the recovered vehicle or replace if total loss occurs. For example, Linda discovered her car is missing. She rents a car to be able to commute to work. Her rental reimbursement limit on the policy is $25 per day. After the police recovered her auto, she returned rental car and paid $250. She rented a vehicle for ten days, but the insurance company will reimburse her only for eight days, for a total of $200.

Having **Loss of Use** coverage is important not just because it will help you get around while your car is in the shop, but it will also make the insurance company to send the check for repairs faster. The longer you drive a rental car, the longer insurance company needs to waste money on rental expenses.

Buying Insurance Policy from the Rental Agency

Many drivers ask themselves if they need to purchase rental insurance or use their own policy. Well, it depends. A passenger auto, trailer, van, or truck not owned by the insured or a family member but used as a substitute for a short time, such as a rental car, is covered under the auto policy. If you have full coverage on your existing auto policy, with high limits and an umbrella policy, you probably can go without purchasing insurance from the rental agency.

Before renting any vehicle, find out what your personal auto policy covers. When you sign the rental agreement, you are taking the responsibility to bring rental car back untouched and in the same condition as the vehicle left the lot. Injuries and property damage that you cause as a driver are covered under your own auto policy liability up to the limits of the coverage. Damages to the rental car that you cause are covered under your auto policy only if you are carrying collision and comprehensive coverage on at least one of your listed vehicles on the policy. Damages to the rental car will be treated the same as damages to your car and are subject to deductibles.

If you do not have comprehensive and collision coverage, you can purchase it from the rental agency. Insurance purchased from a rental agency could cost $15 or more per day. Usually, it comes with limitations that you should read before you drive their car. Some rental places limit their vehicle's driving radius, not permitting it to be driven out of state. It can allow rental vehicle to be driven only by the listed driver and nobody else. It also can exclude careless driving or any losses caused after the driver had a drink.

Depending on the rental company, you can be charged for losses you have no influence on, such as any damages or scratches on your car done by hail, vandalism, another driver not obeying traffic signals, or the car being stolen. In addition, you are responsible for the revenue the rental place is losing while the damaged vehicle is at the shop being repaired. The rental agency cannot charge you the loss of use expense if it has vehicles available for rent.

For example, Tom is on a vacation and rents a Toyota Camry for five days. Unfortunately, on the second day, he gets into an accident by making a wrong turn and rents another vehicle for the rest of his vacation. The rental agency loses four days of rental fees while the Camry is repaired. Fortunately, Tom has a full coverage policy back at home and that takes care of the rental vehicle collision and loss of use expenses. If you don't have such coverage on your policy, you always can purchase it from the rental agency.

If you have an umbrella policy, it can be used to cover any damages to your rental car, even if the rental contract makes you responsible for the damages. In case of an accident, use all other personal auto insurance coverage first. If the losses are so great that your auto policy coverage is not enough, use the umbrella policy as a plan B. To find out more about an umbrella policy, please refer to Chapter 37.

If you have a credit card that promises you to cover your rental car insurance, make sure that it will be counted as primary and will ignore your personal auto insurance. Make sure it does not have any exclusions. Remember, international travel outside the US and Canada and twenty miles away from the US border is not covered under your personal auto policy. Ask about international insurance where you rent the vehicle.

It is good to list anyone involved in renting the car with you on the agreement, such as your brother-in-law or your dearest friend, if you trust him or her. Make sure you are both signing the contract and split the expenses in half. If something happens on the road, you will split the losses in half also. The same approach should be used in renting any other vacation items.

If you are at a conference somewhere and your employer will reimburse expenses for your rental car and insurance, purchase rental insurance separately from your policy. Purchase a separate policy if you had a couple of claims on your current auto policy because adding one more claim would get you into the higher rate zone.

Part VI

Insuring Your Rental Properties

Introduction

Being a landlord and owning a couple of rental properties is a great way to receive monthly income, although it comes with a great responsibility for the dwelling and the renters who live there. If you have a home, condo unit, or townhouse and you are renting it to others, the property needs to be insured with a proper dwelling policy. A dwelling policy is also used for property that does not qualify to be insured under a homeowner's policy because of the age or value of the house.

Chapter 32
Dwelling Policy Forms (DP-1, DP-2, and DP-3)

Usually, dwelling policies insure property rented to others, a tenant-occupied building, or a dwelling under construction. This kind of policy provides coverage for townhouses, row houses, houses with up to five boarders or up to four apartments, and permanently tied down mobile homes. Farms are not covered.

Professional offices, beauty parlors, or photography studios can be insured under this policy as long as the insured conducts operations. The operations conducted on the property have to be a service and would not involve more then three people working at the same time. Since every insurance company has a different take on that, please check with your agent.

A dwelling policy is very similar to a homeowner's policy except many coverage that are automatically included in a homeowner's policy need to be added as an endorsement to a dwelling policy. For example, personal property is not covered under a dwelling policy if it is not added as an endorsement. It can be added at the insured's request for any amount of money—$5,000, $10,000, or more. Because a dwelling policy does not require personal property coverage, some homeowners without much personal property choose an owner–occupied policy. Liability coverage is optional but can be added up to $500,000.

Basic Policy

Basic Policy Coverage, called DP-1 or DP 00 01 form, is a basic coverage package and provides the least amount of coverage. The premium for such a policy is lower than other broader coverage policies. All of us want to save on insurance, but insuring the property at just the minimum is not the answer. If this policy form still looks like it is appropriate for you, you can add endorsements to the policy to add more coverage. Basic form insures against:

- ▶ Fire, lightning, and internal explosion. An internal explosion is typical with a furnace, water heater, or stove. The is no coverage against explosions caused by electrical arching, steam pipes, steam boilers, or breaking relief valves and water pipes. Internal explosions are already covered under basic form, but additional coverage adds coverage for external explosions, even ones that occur in a neighboring property.
- ▶ Wind and hail perils are covered when they enter and damage the insides of the house by making an opening in the roof or window.
- ▶ There is also fire department coverage up to $500 and no deductible if firefighters need to come to protect rental property.

The insured can add the following options:
- ▶ Civil commotion.
- ▶ Riot.
- ▶ Explosion.
- ▶ Smoke.
- ▶ Hail.
- ▶ Windstorm.
- ▶ Volcanic eruption.
- ▶ Vehicles and aircraft. Even if a vehicle or aircraft endorsement is added, loss is not covered if the insured or resident of the rental property causes the loss.

The basic policy does not cover:

► Antennas outside the house
► Signs and awnings
► Fences, walkways, and driveways
► Trees, shrubs, and other plants
► Collapse of the building, glass, or safety glazing that is the part of the building
► Theft losses

An insured can add a vandalism and malicious mischief (V&MM) endorsement. Vandalism coverage cannot be applied to a building vacant for more than sixty consecutive days.

After damage occurs to the dwelling, the insured's responsibility is to protect the rest of the property from damage. If there are simple, reasonable repairs being done to the dwelling, those will be covered under the policy. For example, an explosion made a hole in the wall. Kenny paid for the wall to be boarded up to protect the rest of the belongings inside. The insurance company will reimburse these expenses. Debris removal pays to remove debris from the covered peril.

Worldwide coverage provides 10 percent of the Coverage C limit for personal property that can be located anywhere in the world. Property removed from the dwelling to protect it from perils under the policy also covered, but only for five days.

Broad Policy

Broad Policy Coverage, DP-2 or DP 00 02, provides a broader version of the previously mentioned basic form. The broad policy also covers named perils, such as a dwelling, other structures, and personal property. In addition to DP-1 coverages, DP-2 adds more coverage and is better for owner-occupied policies. The following items are additional coverage:

► Damage caused by a burglar, not including theft. The property should not be vacant for more than thirty days to be insured for theft coverage.

▶ Falling objects; weight of ice, sleet, or snow.

▶ Freezing of the plumbing, air conditioning units, heating, protective fire sprinkler systems, and household appliances are covered, although the insured needs to drain the plumbing and keep the heat in the dwelling to prevent the freezing of the plumbing.

▶ Sudden discharge of water or stream and the cracking and tearing apart of heating units in the house are covered.

▶ Sudden and accidental damage of discharge from artificially created electrical current is covered, although it does not include damage to a transistor or similar electrical component.

▶ The vehicles peril covers damage that occurred by somebody else but not the insured driving into the building, fence, or driveway. It covers damage when the insured or a resident of the insured household damages somebody else's property. For example, if your drunk neighbor Dayton could not control a vehicle and crashed into your fence, your policy will cover that.

▶ Damage caused by fireplace smoke.

▶ Broken glass or safety glazing material that is part of the building, storm door, or window.

The following items are not covered:

▶ Damage to a building's contents or its interiors is covered only if a falling object first damaged the roof before falling inside the building.

▶ Awnings, fences, pavements and patios, docks, wharves, bulkheads, foundations, and swimming pools.

▶ Outside television and radio antennas, towers, mats, piers, and lead-in wire are not covered from damage caused by wind, snow, sleet, or ice.

▶ Lawns, shrubs, trees, and plants.

▶ If the building was vacant for more than sixty consecutive days, burglar and accidental discharge perils are also not covered.

► If an accidental overflow or discharge was continuous, or the unit had repeated leakage or freezing and damaged the appliances, the peril is not covered.

Special Policy

Special Policy Coverage, DP-3 or DP00 03, is the most complete coverage of all dwelling policy forms. This form provides open peril coverage on the dwelling and other structures that include all physical loss unless it is specifically excluded in the policy. Personal property is covered the same as DP-2, broad form, on a named peril basis.

► If the damage is caused by water that is not from heating, cooling, air conditioning, sprinkler systems, or plumbing, replacement or repair for the damaged part of the building is covered. But it would not cover the repair of the system or appliance.

► Collapse pays for dwelling collapse caused by a specified limit of perils that cause an abrupt cave-in, rendering part of the building unlivable. If the cause was insect or vermin damage that insured knew about, the damage is not covered.

► Glass or safety glazing material is covered if the damage is caused by glass breakage from part of the residential structure, storm windows, and doors.

► Damage to foundation, walls, floor, or ceilings made by settling, bulging, expanding, or dispersal is not covered.

► Freezing of plumbing, air conditioning, automatic protective fire sprinkler system, heating system, or household appliances are not covered by the policy.

► Wear and tear, deterioration, mechanical breakdown, corrosion, rust, mold, wet or dry rot, smog from smudging, or industrial operations are excluded.

► Discharge, slow seepage, or escape of pollutants such as smoke, soot, fumes, vapor, alkali, and chemicals and waste are not covered.

► Damages from birds, insects, domestic animals, or vermin are not covered.

- ► The insurance company usually won't pay more than $500 for damage to any one tree, shrub, or bush.
- ► The ordinance of law coverage pays up to 10 percent of the Coverage A limit of liability to repair or replace a building or other structure. In the DP-2 and DP-3 forms, property removed from the location is covered for thirty days.

Exclusions for All Forms

- ► Losses from earth movements, land shockwave, tremors, mudslides, or sinkholes are not covered by a dwelling policy.
- ► Any water damage, such as flooding, and any water that is leaking or seeping from the ground or is caused by weather conditions, a sump pump, or other equipment is excluded.
- ► Losses from a power interruption that occurs away from the building, neglect, intentional loss, losses caused by war, nuclear hazard, government or public authority seizure of property, or faulty or defective items.
- ► If damage occurred and the insured did not protect the property from additional loss, the additional loss is not covered.

Endorsements

There are endorsements that can be added to the policy to provide more coverage.

- ► An **automatic increase in insurance** endorsement provides an annual increase in Coverage A (dwelling) and Coverage B (other structures) by 4 percent, 6 percent, or 8 percent of the dwelling limit. Under this endorsement, the policy limits will increase annually by a percentage the insured chooses. This coverage is prorated. Let's say the policy is effective for half of the policy period. Then half of the annual increase is applied.
- ► A **dwelling under construction** endorsement provides coverage to the dwelling being constructed. Usually, dwelling policies do not cover vacant dwellings. The amount insured on any date is calcu-

lated by a percentage of the provisional amount between the actual dwelling value on the given date and the day of the completion.

► A **broad theft endorsement** covers owner-occupied personal property and is an additional coverage next to personal property coverage. This endorsement covers perils such as on- and off-premises theft, attempted theft, vandalism, and malicious mischief. There is no coverage if the property is vacant for more than thirty consecutive days before the loss occurs. To find out more about this endorsement, ask your agent.

Chapter 33

Dwelling Coverage

All forms of dwelling insurance have four main parts.
- ▶ Coverage A covers the dwelling itself.
- ▶ Coverage B covers other structures.
- ▶ Coverage C covers personal property.
- ▶ Coverage D insures fair rental value.

A policy can consist of all four parts, and insurers prefer to write them that way, although the insured can decide what coverage to keep and what coverage to remove. Let's say Mariana rents a house and purchases a DP-3 policy. She doesn't have any personal property on the premises, so she excludes this coverage and saves money on the premium.

Other coverage parts can be added to the policy per the insured's request:
- ▶ Coverage E for loss of use
- ▶ Coverage L for personal liability
- ▶ Coverage M for medical payments

Coverage A, Dwelling

Coverage A covers the dwelling itself and structures attached to the dwelling, such as an attached garage or porch. It covers outdoor equipment used to service the dwelling, such as a lawnmower to cut the grass. Construction materials used to repair the dwelling and stored on the premises are also covered. This coverage does not apply to land that the property is located on. Dwelling limits are determined by using a replacement cost estimator, same as a homeowner's policy, by calculating how much it would cost to rebuild the dwelling in case of a total loss. Your agent should be familiar with regionally adjusted construction cost guides and can recommend the dwelling limits that you need.

Coverage B, Other Structures

Coverage B covers other structures on the premises not attached to the building that have a clear space between the building and structure or are connected to the main dwelling only by fence, plumbing, or utility line. Other structures include a detached garage or storage sheds where equipment to service the property is held. The structure can't contain any liquid fuel or store gaseous hazards. Mausoleums or grave markers are not covered under a dwelling policy; they are only covered under a homeowner's policy.

Usually, by default, many insurance companies set the Coverage B insurable limit at only 10 percent of the dwelling limit. If you have a guesthouse, apartment above your garage, or other structure on your premises with a higher than normal value, you should notify your agent. Describe the structure in detail and how much you think it would cost to rebuild it in case of a total loss. Coverage B limits can be increased per an insured's request to the amount that would be enough to rebuild the structure.

Coverage C, Personal Property

Coverage C covers the insured's personal property on the premises. There is a big difference between a homeowner's policy and a dwelling policy in regards to the personal property coverage. If the property is rented out, and the insured doesn't live in the house, many times the insured declines personal property coverage altogether. If you decide to do the same, make sure you are not leaving behind the refrigerator, washer and dryer or other appliances in your rental property. Losing them can cost you up to a couple of thousand dollars.

Other exclusions include:

▶ A tenant's personal property. The tenant should have his or her own policy to cover personal items. But the insured can request that personal property belonging to a tenant or his guests be added to the Coverage C.

▶ Anything insured by another policy is excluded under Coverage C.

▶ Money, credit cards, currency, bank notes, securities, evidences of debt, gold medals, silver or other metals are not covered.

▶ Intellectual property items, such as manuscripts, drawings, or other paper records.

▶ Computer equipment, such as discs, software, records, and electronic data.

▶ Animals, birds, and fish kept on the property.

▶ Any aircrafts, boats, or other motor vehicles are not covered and should have a separate policy. Only model planes or hobby aircraft can be covered.

▶ Mail or property being shipped needs insurance from the post office.

▶ Property that is to be sold or delivered, samples of property being sold, business property, or an employee working at the insured house are not covered.

Please check with your agent for more information on your rental property coverage and exclusions. Many policies are different.

Coverage D, Loss of rent

Coverage D is used to reimburse any lost rental revenue to the insured of the rental property. This coverage is highly recommended in case something happens to the rental property. Let's say the dishwasher breaks and ruins the carpet, which needs to be replaced. While repairs are done to the property, a tenant cannot live there and temporarily moves out. The insurance company covers the rent for the months that the tenant doesn't live on the premises and doesn't pay the rent. It is important to mention this coverage to your agent when getting a quote and name the amount that will be reimbursed per month.

Coverage E, Loss of Use

Coverage E covers loss of use expenses, such as additional living expenses to maintain a normal standard of living. If the dwelling has been damaged, and the insured needs to move to a hotel temporarily until the residence is proper to live in again, the loss of use coverage will cover any restaurant, dry cleaning, and transportation expenses.

Coverage L, Personal Liability, and Coverage M, Medical

Coverage L provides coverage for bodily injury and property damage losses that other person incurred because of the insured's actions. The insurance company provides coverage even for fraudulent or groundless claims. It also pays for bodily injury and personal property loss as well as payoffs and fees associated with lawsuits. Coverage can be as low as $5,000 or as high as $500,000. For example, let's say Erwin is recovering after surgery, and his friends are visiting him. Erwin's friend's son steals a painkiller bottle and then dies at home later from an overdose. The father of the son sues Erwin. All the expenses associated with court will be covered.

Coverage M covers medical payments to others caused by the insured's activities for up to three years after the loss occurred. It covers doctor's visits, X-rays, and other expenses. This coverage takes care of injuries caused to the other person while visiting the insured's property with the insured's permission. It also covers losses from an animal that the insured owns or had in his or her care at the time of the accident. Depending on the policy, this coverage can be up to $10,000 per person, and it is paid by insurance company even if the insured is not legally liable for the accident.

Additional coverage applies to the damage to property of others, up to $500 or replacement cost. First aid to others and claim expenses are also covered. For example, Violet invites guests to the party, but someone cuts her finger helping Violet cook dinner. The injured person is rushed to the emergency room for medical help. Let's say the total medical bills for the accident come to $1,400, but Violet's medical payment limit is $1,000. Because it is a first aid expense, it will be paid in addition to the limit of liability, and the whole expense will be covered.

This coverage includes defense and court costs charged against the insured in any suit, as well as premiums on bonds that are required as long as it doesn't exceed the coverage limit. It also covers $50 per day for lost earnings if the insured is helping the insurer at the insurer's request, as well as reasonable expenses incurred by the insured and post-judgment interest.

Exclusions

- Accidents caused by the insured to another insured's family member.
- Losses caused by insured.
- War.
- Business pursuits or failure to render professional services.
- Use, sale, or possession of controlled substances or other prescription drugs.
- Sexual molestation.
- Physical and mental abuse.
- Transmission of a communicable disease.
- Rental of a premises that are not covered.
- Ownership or loading of a watercraft or vehicles.
- Damage to the property owned by the insured.
- Damage to property rented to, used by, or occupied by insured. It is covered only in a case of fire, smoke, or explosion.
- Anything that can be covered under other insurance, like workers' compensation.

▶ Loss assessments charged against the insured if the insured is a member of an association, community, or corporation, assumed under most contract and agreements.

▶ Injury to the insured or a minor who lives in the same household.

Coverage M excludes the following:

▶ The employee who works for the insured but at the time of loss was outside the insured's property and the injury is not associated with work performed at the insured's location.

▶ Nuclear hazard.

▶ Any person other than a residence employee who regularly lives on insured's location.

Part VII

Additional insurance policies

Introduction

Unfortunately, having home and auto policies alone are not enough to have full coverage. The things you own, the more you need to insure. Having an umbrella policy that gives additional liability coverage anywhere in the world is a good idea and is not only for the rich. Recreational vehicles, boats, and other toys should carry separate, specialized insurance policies. It is assumed some insurance coverage is included in a homeowner's policy, but some items should be insured separately. Flood policies are an example of this.

Chapter 34
Recreational Vehicles

Recreational vehicles are usually used for fun and relaxation. Recreational vehicles include:

Boats

- ► Snowmobiles
- ► Golf carts
- ► Moto-cross bikes
- ► All-terrain vehicles
- ► Mopeds
- ► Personal watercrafts such as jet skis
- ► Motor homes
- ► Caravans

Although such vehicles are used not that often, maybe a couple of times a year, it can bring the same heavy risk for injuries or property damage to others while operating such vehicles.

Owning a Recreational Vehicle

Usually, recreational vehicles are not for a regular road use and should be insured separately. Most of the time, anything that has a motor, except service vehicles like lawn mowers, are excluded from the homeowner's policy. Some homeowner's policies can provide liability coverage for borrowed or rented recreational vehicles, such as snowmobiles in Utah or a golf cart at your local golf club.

Some homeowner's policies started covering golf cart driving in retirement communities if there is necessity and it is allowed by the homeowner's association. To be sure about what your policy covers, contact your agent.

An umbrella policy gives you additional liability coverage on recreational vehicles, but it will not cover collision or comprehensive damages and will not cover towing and labor. Insuring the property properly will save you from costly damage repairs from your own pocket.

If you own a recreational vehicle, the coverage can be purchased as a standalone recreational vehicle policy. Others can be added as an endorsement to your homeowner's or auto policies.

Trailers

Trailers are used for everything and come in every size, shape, and color. Your auto policy will extend the liability coverage to the trailer while vehicle is attached to it. The moment the trailer is unattached, your homeowner's policy can pick up liability if it is at your residence or a temporary location, such as a campground.

If a camping trailer is on land that you lease, such as a trailer park lot leased for the summer, you can get an extension on your homeowner's policy. That way you will provide the liability coverage to the trailer and the lot itself.

An auto policy can cover the collision and comprehensive coverage on your trailer by adding a special endorsement. Personal property in the trailer is covered under the homeowner's policy as off-premises property. You also can add additional coverage for breakage. But if you parked your trailer on a lot owned or rented long term, such as a lakeshore lot, there is no theft coverage when you are not there.

Motor Home

A motor home can be insured under your personal auto policy by endorsement or separately. Motor homes carry a higher risk than a regular vehicle. Using any recreational vehicle creates a risk for personal injuries, collisions, thefts of personal property, and vandalism. In addition to those risks, other things can go wrong with the unit and cost money, such as appliance malfunctions or plumbing and electrical system problems. Purchasing additional, more specialized insurance to cover a motor home will give you peace of mind, insure personal things, provide towing and labor coverage, and even replace your motor home in case of total loss. If you are renting a motor home, purchase additional insurance provided by the rental place and read everything about that policy.

Renting a Recreational Vehicle

If you are renting a recreational vehicle, the liability coverage from your policy will cover only the other person's bodily injury and property damage if the accident is your fault.

The damages to a rental vehicle itself are not covered under your policy, so it is important to purchase rental insurance that would provide the coverage no matter whose fault it is. There is confusion about the deposit you leave when renting a recreation vehicle. Many believe that a $500 deposit will cover any damage cost to the rental property. It is true when the damage is less than the deposit. If the damage is bigger—let's say the engine burns, which is more than the deposit—you will be responsible for replacing it.

When renting any recreational vehicles, be careful about who signs the contract. The person who signs the contract is the person responsible for the damaged rental. Even if you split the deposit in half with your friend, but only you signed it, the rental agency will go after you personally for the damage.

If you own any recreational vehicles or are renting one, you should have an umbrella policy, which is discussed in Chapter 37.

Chapter 35
Personal Watercraft

I f you have a boat with an outboard motor of twenty-five horsepower or less or a sailboat that is less than twenty-six feet long, your liability is included on your homeowner's policy. If you have other boats or jet skis, you will need to buy a separate broad liability policy or add an endorsement to your homeowner's policy. To be sure, please check with your agent.

Liability coverage on a homeowner's policy is excluded for boats with motors of twenty-five horsepower or more, and for boats more than twenty-six feet long. For those who own bigger boats, you need to purchase specialized policies, such as watercraft policies, inland marine forms, or ocean marine policies.

Even with a watercraft policy, there are limitations. It covers only boats used for personal pleasure and can't transport people for a fee or be used for businesses, hired out, rented out, or chartered. In addition, if the watercraft is being used in an official race or speed contest, it is excluded; unofficial events are not excluded. Obviously, no drinking and driving is allowed on a boat, and damages made to others by the insured can be excluded. Wear and tear and maintenance are excluded.

For the boats not owned or rented, let's say they're borrowed, the homeowner's policy will cover liability losses. For example, your friend invites you to ski, and he asks you to drive while he is skiing. If something happens, your homeowner's insurance will cover it. If you are holding the helm of the sailboat because your friend asked you to, and you collide with the other boat, your homeowner's insurance will cover that too.

If you rent a boat on vacation, your homeowner's policy covers liability, except for boats more than twenty-six feet long or with a motor of more than fifty horsepower. To get insurance coverage for the boats excluded on homeowner's policy, you can buy coverage from the rental place. If you already have a boat liability policy, you can add the covered to rented boats.

There are different types of watercraft insurance.

▶ **Boat owner's/watercraft package** policies include combined property, liability, and medical payments insurance on an open peril basis. It used to insure boats under a specified length, such boats less than thirty feet long, or under a maximum dollar value, such as less than $25,000. Losses can be paid by actual cash value or endorsed to be insured for an agreed amount.

▶ **Outboard motor and boat** insurance can be written to cover the physical damage exposure of boats. It is covered under open peril inland marine floaters. This kind insurance covers motors, motor boats, trailers, and accessories. It provides a very limited coverage for collision damage to another vessel, and losses are paid on actual cash value. It is customary for the owner of the vessel to have liability coverage under a homeowner's policy or a separate liability umbrella policy.

▶ **Personal yacht policies** are ocean marine forms that provide a package of property and liability coverage. Large pleasure boats, such as sailboats with inboard auxiliary power and inboard boats are insured under this policy. Smaller boats also can be covered if they are in good condition and have some value. Coverage is usually limited to property coverage on the hull, with or without coverage for a trailer. Liability is covered under homeowner's or a separate liability umbrella policy. Owners of larger vessels can purchase the complete package of yacht coverage, which includes hull insurance (parts replacement cost for partial losses and on a valued basis for total losses) and boat trailer insurance (which pays on an actual cash value basis). This package includes protection and indemnity, bodily injury, and property damage liability insurance; medical payments coverage; and federal long-shore and harbor worker's compensation insurance, which provides benefits for maritime workers. All coverages are provided on an open peril basis.

▶ **Hull coverage** on a yacht policy contains a collision clause, which covers the insured's liability for collision damage to other vessels. This is an additional amount of insurance, and it is equal to the amount of coverage written on the hull. Protection and indemnity (P&I) coverage for collision damage to another vessel begins after the insurance provided by the collision clause is exhausted.

▶ **A water skiing clause** commonly excludes coverage for people skiing or otherwise being towed by the vessel until they are back on board or have landed safely.

▶ **The layup warranty** applies when the yacht is located in a safe berth for storage and is not being used, such as during the winter months. It provides for a return of premium because it reduces risk of loss.

▶ Every yacht policy has **navigational limits**, a clause that defines an area in which the yacht is permitted to operate. Losses that occur outside these limits are not covered unless the insurer has granted permission for the insured to operate in those areas.

When buying free-standing boat policy, make sure you include the boat, motor, and trailer, because they can be stolen separately. Make sure you insure it with enough coverage on agreed value basis to buy a new boat at the retail price, including taxes. Also, add additional equipment coverage for a couple of hundred dollars for things like life jackets, anchor, oars, fuel tanks, seat cushions, and so on.

To reduce the premium, some insurance companies give a discount for boating safety class that has been approved by US Coast Guard. Please check with your agent.

Anyone operating a watercraft should have umbrella policy. To find out more about umbrella policy, please read Chapter 37.

Chapter 36
Flood Insurance

F lood insurance is one of those additional insurance policies that nobody wants to waste money on, especially if the property is not located in the flood zone. It is hard to imagine a street flooding when it has not flooded in the last twenty years. It is hard to imagine flood damaging your personal property while in a drought.

Unfortunately, many homeowners are left with unpaid claims by their homeowner's insurance, just to find out that flooding is not covered under their homeowner's policy. We all think about purchasing flood insurance when the tropical storm is pouring down or when the local river is swollen near our house. That is not a time to purchase flood insurance, and no insurance company will sell you a policy when a hurricane is in the Gulf of Mexico or when you are evacuating. Purchasing flood insurance gives you peace of mind like any other insurance and needs to be purchased ahead of time.

What Is a Flood?

A **flood** is defined as an overflow of inland or tidal waters, a collapse of a land because of excessive erosion due to flood, mudslides caused by accumulations of water on the ground or underground, or usual and rapid accumulation or runoff of surface water from any source, unless general flooding exists. Sewer backup into a dwelling is not covered.

Floods are very common in the areas prone to tropical rains and hurricanes and in areas where rivers absorb melting snow during spring. Flash rains after the drought cause floods mostly because dry land takes more time to absorb the rain. Old subdivisions with clogged storm drains are more prone to flooding. New subdivisions also can have clogged water drainage due to the construction debris in the street. A new subdivision in the area will increase possibility of a flood. A meadow or a forest absorbs the water very well. If we built a town covered in cement with buildings and streets, rainwater has nowhere to go and floods the streets.

How to Get Flood Insurance

Flood insurance was unavailable up until 1968, when Congress created the National Flood Insurance Program (NFIP) to make flood insurance available to the eligible communities through federal subsidization. The program is managed by the Federal Insurance Administration (FIA), which is a branch of the Federal Emergency Management Agency (FEMA). In most cases, communities voluntarily apply for the coverage. Any building on a permanent site, above the ground, walled and roofed, is eligible for the flood insurance.

There are two types of flood programs: emergency and regular. **Emergency programs** go into effect when the community applies to the NFIP and remains in effect until the government finalizes the flood insurance rates for that community. Under the emergency program, the insured may purchase limited amounts of flood insurance for buildings and contents at subsidized rates. After the **regular program** goes into effect, additional coverage may be purchased.

NFIP policies may be sold by private insurance companies through the FIA's "Write Your Own" program. Under this system, the FIA sets rates, eligibility requirements, and coverage limitations. The participating company collects the premiums and pays for the losses out of these premiums. If the insurance company collects more in premiums than it pays out in losses, the excess must be returned to the government. Most of the time, the insurance companies that sell flood insurance also sell homeowner's, dwelling, and other policies.

For the flood coverage to go into effect, an application for the NFIP must be completed and accompanied by the gross policy premium payment in full. Payment cannot be divided into partial payments, and no payment plan is available. After the payment is received, there is a thirty-day waiting period for the policy to go into effect. The waiting period is waved only if you are buying a house and need to submit all insurance supporting proof at the time of a closing. If your new home is not in a flood zone and your mortgage does not require flood insurance, don't expect them to pay for your flood insurance from your escrow account. If flood insurance is required, you can request a payment to be released from your escrow account, same as your hazard insurance.

Don't think that flood insurance is included in your homeowner's policy, and that purchasing a flood policy is like doubly insuring the property. If you are not sure if you need flood insurance, check with the agent who takes care of your homeowner's policy. You also should check flood zone maps and request an elevation certificate to determine if your house is in a flood zone. Every couple of years, flood zone maps are redrawn and corrected. If you are in a flood zone, your mortgagee will require you to purchase flood insurance. If you don't have a mortgagee, and you are the owner of your house, check with your agent every year to make sure you are not in a flood zone.

To purchase flood insurance, you don't have to be in the flood zone. If you are not in the flood zone, and you want to insure your property just in case of a flood, you will be charged a preferred rate. This type of coverage is very affordable; the premium is a couple of hundred dollars a year.

A flood emergency insurance program covers the buildings up to $35,000 and the contents up to $10,000. The preferred program covers the building up to $250,000, with personal property coverage up to $100,000. Both building and personal coverage have deductibles. The standard deductible for each coverage is $1,000 under the emergency program and $500 under the regular program. The deductibles are applied separately for building and contents per occurrence. Deductibles can vary and can be increased or decreased by the insured upon request.

If your property is located in a flood zone, it is subject to standard flood policy premium rates, which are higher than preferred rate premiums.

Let's say you have a house, and you have a homeowner's policy and a flood insurance policy. If you decide to sell the house, you can do it in two different ways with the flood coverage. You can cancel the policy, providing HUD statements and receiving a refund, or you can assign flood coverage to the new owner of the house. The flood insurance can be assigned to the other insured with the title of the property. Some insurance companies request written consent from the previous insured, and some don't.

What Flood Insurance Covers

Depending on the insured's request, a flood policy can cover the dwelling with the content or just the contents. If you own a home, you should purchase both. If you rent the apartment or a house, you can purchase only the personal property flood coverage. A flood policy covers the property in the policy description against direct loss by or from flood. Indirect financial loss or expenses resulted out of the premises being unlivable are not covered. Property is also covered outside the premises, outside of the special flood hazard area, for forty-five days when removed by the insured to protect it from a flood.

For example, Lee knows that a flood warning is issued, and he transports most of his personal property to his brother's house, who to lives upstate. This personal property is stored in the brother's garage and will be covered by Lee's policy.

Single-family dwellings other than mobile homes are the only buildings that may be insured with a replacement cost. It is automatically provided when the building is insured for at least 80 percent of its replacement value or for the maximum amount of insurance allowed by the flood program. All other losses are paid on an actual cash value basis, such as personal property. Debris removal expenses are covered if the expenses plus the direct loss do not exceed the policy limit.

A flood policy does not cover:

- Underground structures and equipment, such as wells and septic tanks
- Newly constructed buildings that are in, on, or over the water
- Fences
- Retaining walls
- Outdoor swimming pools
- Bulkheads, wharves, piers, bridges, docks, and other open structures on or over water
- Aircraft, motor vehicles, and self-propelled vehicles
- Structures that are primarily containers, such as gas or liquid storage, silos, grain storage buildings, or their contents
- Lawns, plants, trees, shrubs, livestock, and growing crops

To find out more about flood program, please go to www.floodsmart. gov or contact your agent.

Chapter 37
Umbrella Policy

These days, anyone can be sued for almost anything. If you caused a six-car accident on the road because you were texting, you can be sued. If you had a party in your home and somebody tripped on that staircase that you had no time to fix, you can be sued. The court can order your personal savings and personal property to be taken away from you. Even your future earnings can be subject to paying for loss. That is why it is very important to have at least a $1 million umbrella policy.

An **umbrella** policy provides additional liability insurance over and above the basic coverage provided by underlying liability insurance, such as an auto policy. It also covers some losses excluded by the auto or homeowner's liability insurance.

It provides coverage against lawsuits that insured, dependent of the insured, or even a pet caused bodily injury or property damage to other person by accident. False claims, false arrests, slander, libel, vandalism, and more are covered. An umbrella policy covers the insured and his or her family anywhere in the world. Any insured with teenage drivers in the household should consider this coverage as a necessity. If you own a couple houses, and rent some houses out or have a dog, a boat, or a Jet Ski, you should have umbrella policy. The more property you own, the more risk you are taking.

Although coverage limits for a personal umbrella policy range from $1 million to $5 million, the premiums are not that high. The majority of a loss is paid by your primary auto insurance, so your umbrella insurance rates are not that expensive. An umbrella policy can cost between $110 to $300 per year, depending on how much property it covers. If you are a politician, movie star, or other public figure, your umbrella policy should be purchased with an insurance company that specializes in those kinds of umbrella policies.

For an example of how an umbrella policy works, let's say Bonny has an auto policy with $100,000 liability limit. She causes a big accident and is sued. Luckily, she has umbrella policy with $1 million coverage. The court orders her to pay $500,000 in losses. When the auto liability limit is exhausted, the umbrella policy kicks in to pay for the rest.

Usually an umbrella is written with an underlying auto policy. Depending on the insurance company, the limits on the auto policy can start as low as $250,000 and go up to $500,000. When altering auto policy liability limits, keep in mind that you should not go lower than the required limit to use an umbrella policy. If you have an auto policy limit up to $250,000 and you lower the limit to $200,000, one day, when you want to use umbrella coverage, you notice that there is a $50,000 gap. You will need to pay that gap out of your own pocket to reach that $250,000 limit, when the umbrella policy can kick in.

Even an umbrella policy has exclusions, such as liability covered under workers' compensation, acts that made intentionally by the insured, liability arising out of business pursuits, or punitive damages against you. When loss is excluded under an underlying policy and umbrella policy, there is no coverage at all, and the insured is personally responsible to pay for the damage.

If you have an umbrella policy with an underlying personal auto policy, and you don't have the auto policy anymore, you still can keep your umbrella policy by purchasing nonowner auto insurance policy with 500 CSL limits. You also can purchase a standalone excess liability policy that does not require an underlying policy. Please contact your agent to decide which policy will be best for you.

Bibliography

Hunglemann, Jack. *Insurance for Dummies, 2nd Ed*. Hoboken, NJ: Wiley Publishing Inc., 2009

    Weiss Ratings Consumer Guide to Homeowners Insurance. Palm Beach Gardens, FL: Weiss Ratings, 2003

    Zevnik, Richard W. *The Complete Book of Insurance*. Naperville, IL: Sphinx Publishing, 2004

Index

townhouse, 55, 65, 93, 96, 99, 100, 165

trailer, 78, 128, 133, 137, 162, 184, 189

trial, 114

U

umbrella policy, 16, 82, 130, 137, 162, 163, 181, 184, 185, 188, 189, 190, 197, 198

uninsured/underinsured motorists, 136

V

vandalism or malicious mischief, 90, 106

vehicle, 5, 20, 25, 26, 29, 76, 78, 86, 90, 107, 115, 117, 118, 119, 120, 125, 127, 128, 129, 130, 131, 132, 133, 136, 137, 138, 139, 140, 141, 142, 143, 144, 145, 146, 150, 151, 152, 154, 155, 156, 157, 161, 162, 163, 164, 168, 170, 184, 185

W

watercraft, 40, 76, 86, 87, 179, 187, 188, 190

Made in the USA
Las Vegas, NV
26 July 2021